Praise for Overdue Heresies

Malcolm's observations are thoughtful and well informed, challenging both stifling orthodoxy and the bogus argumentation of those who use the very science which Malcolm sees as revealing Divine methodology to promote 'randomality'. Perhaps, only a Quaker bound by no orthodoxy and an attorney schooled in open mindedness could have penned these observations

—Phil Megna

Malcolm Bell, having absorbed the teaching of his childhood's church, has spent much of his adult life trying to align those teachings with truths he has gleaned from science and his own experience. As a Quaker, he accepts the idea that Truth gained from meditation and personal seeking is to be trusted and followed. His book invites its readers into their own personal seeking after Truth.

—Mary Eagleson

With a wry sense of humor, Quaker philosopher and theologian Malcolm Bell has created an entirely fresh daybook for the reader to savor and enjoy.

Like a companionable pair of really good, broken-in garden gloves, daybooks are a special part of the contemplative life and like others of this genre, Bell's *Overdue Heresies* is meant to be used. Grab a handful of bookmarks and a sharp pencil before you start to read as you will find yourself wanting to go back again and again to thoughtfully provoking reflections. Go ahead and scribble in the margins your own responses to the quandaries and moral dilemmas the author has placed in your lap. If you're like me, you'll want to put Bell's book on your breakfast table where you can read a paragraph each day with your first cuppa.

Bell's writing style is clear and concise. His logic honed to a keen edge that delights as it lays bare fresh approaches to complex issues confronting contemporary society.

—Len Cadwallader, former Presiding Clerk of Hanover (NH) Friends Meeting

Overdue Heresies presents Malcolm Bell's clear-headed insights, humble humanity, and deep love for God behind all his questions in a way that rings true for this moment in time. As more and more of us abandon institutional religion for more liberating spiritualities, I find Bell provides gravitas and grace to our quest.

—The Rev. Dr. James Lumsden, Spiritual Director

Malcolm's reflections are deep, probing, and thoughtful. I highly recommend you give them some space to ponder your own thoughts on God, life, and goodness.

—Peter J Nagle, M.A.R.

This is an interesting and thought-provoking book by an older American who looks back on his years of religion and practice, and raises questions at variance with some of today's religions. His insight and willingness to examine alternative views is refreshing.

Mr. Bell, a well-educated and widely read individual, reviews a number of tenets of modern religions, and tries to bring religious teachings into line with modern science and observations. He is a deeply religious and spiritual individual who became a Quaker after a more traditional Christian upbringing.

The author begins by contrasting the Big Bang theory with the teachings of Genesis in the Bible. Can evolution be completely explained by a chance combination of circumstances for elements to form on Earth, gradually, or was the hand of a Creator involved?

Many issues reviewed in the book will cause readers to pause and reflect on whatever form religion may have taken in their own lives, and reach conclusions at variance with accepted lessons from the Bible, Scripture, and religious leaders.

I recommend the book to those who seek new perspectives on their own beliefs.

—Peter Areson, M.D.

Malcolm Bell has been a careful and conscientious custodian of his long spiritual life and growth. In *Overdue Heresies* he offers the reader his clear-minded synthesis with numerous examples drawn not only from his own life, but also from the collective and individual lives he's observed during his spiritual journey, activist engagement, and wide reading. I read it slowly to allow for contemplation in the Quaker way of Minding the Light.

—Carl Buffum

Malcolm's heresies remind me of Jesus' blasphemous encounter with the woman at the well. What at first may seem sacrilegious: holds the opportunity for Faith-filled growth.

—Michael Barszewski

How did Malcolm happen to write down so many things that I had been thinking?

—Mary Ann Cadwallader, former Presiding Clerk of Hanover (NH) Friends Meeting

Throughout his life, Malcolm Bell has been questioning his religion, seeking answers and figuring out how to apply his beliefs to his life. As a boy he decided that portions of his Episcopal faith did not make sense to him. As an adult he became a Quaker. Now he has collected many of his thoughts on topics ranging from God to miracles to forgiveness to the afterlife to war. Quakers will find his thoughts inspirational and may help them focus during Meeting. Others who are seeking to clarify their beliefs will be rewarded by Malcolm's approach to important questions.

— Andrew Thompson

This is not like a hard-driving detective story that you gallop through to get to the (often implausible) answer to the key question of 'whodunnit?' Joining Malcom Bell for 'Overdue Heresies' is more like a ramble through familiar countryside on a summer's day; countryside that somehow seems new and fresh because of the wry observations, open-ended musings, and shrewd, challenging questions of an old and trusted friend. Following the advice of Friends to take life 'seriously, but not in deadly earnest,' Bell invites us to join him—for a short walk, or a longer hike, the choice is yours—as he ponders weighty questions of faith (God, Sin, Salvation), or religious practice (Prophesy, Prayer), or social issues (War, Suffering), or just the perplexing exasperating and sometimes exhilarating challenges of living (People). It is an impressive book and one that I enjoy diving back into when I am ready for another walk and challenging conversation with an old friend.

—Michael Morfit, Co-Clerk of Wilderness Friends Meeting of Shrewsbury, VT

Throughout his life, Malcolm Bell has been questioning his religion, seeking answers and figuring out how to apply his beliefs to his life. As a boy he decided that portions of his Episcopal faith did not make sense to him. As an adult he became a Quaker. Now he has collected many of his thoughts on topics ranging from God to miracles to forgiveness to the afterlife to war. Quakers will find his thoughts inspirational and may help them focus during Meeting. Others who are seeking to clarify their beliefs will be rewarded by Malcolm's approach to important questions.

—David Martin, Co-Clerk of Wilderness Friends Meeting of Shrewsbury, VT

OVERDUE HERESIES

Books by Malcolm Bell

The Turkey Shoot: Tracking the Attica Cover-up
Grove Press, 1985
reissued as

The Attica Turkey Shoot: Carnage, Cover-up and the Pursuit of Justice
Skyhorse Publishing, 2017, paperback, 2022

Roses in the Night: Mayan Sisters Confront CIA-Backed Terror
Fresh Look Press, 2023

OVERDUE HERESIES
AND THE SEARCH FOR TRUTH

Malcolm Bell

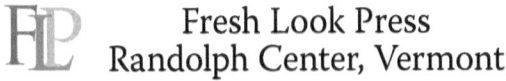
Fresh Look Press
Randolph Center, Vermont

Overdue Heresies and the Search for Truth

Malcolm Bell

Fresh Look Press

Randolph Center, Vermont

freshlookpress.com

Cover art: "Mary of the Cosmos" Copyright © 2004 Bernadette Bostwick of Green Mountain Monastery and the Thomas Berry Sanctuary of Greensboro, Vermont. Sister Bernadette's permission to use this art does not mean that She agrees with anything written in this book or even that she has read it.

Author photo: Bob Aldrich

Book design by Kitty Werner, RSBPress, Waitsfield, Vermont

Library of Congress Control Number: 2024911899

ISBN 979-8-9889080-4-3   tradepaper
ISBN 979-8-9889080-5-0   ebook

For Nancy

It is my fondest hope that we shall remain together hereafter.

"Nothing gives rest but the sincere search for truth."
— Blaise Pascal

"This hour in history needs a dedicated circle of transformed nonconformists."
— Rev. Martin Luther King, Jr.

"Jesus subverted the conventional wisdom of his time. We have to do the same."
— Rev. William Sloane Coffin

"In the twenty-first century, the religious agenda will be set not by tradition's answers but by congregant's questions."
— Rabbi Harold S. Kushner

"There is a crack in everything… That's how the light gets in."
—Leonard Cohen

"Keep the company of people who seek the truth; run from those who have found it."
— Vaclav Havel

Contents

Author's Note

This book offers one person's reflections about God, the cosmos, and people. It challenges many points of Christian doctrine. I hope it will prompt readers to review, articulate, or form their own thoughts about these subjects. Though I call myself a seeker, I do not seek to convince anyone of anything. Indeed, I encourage readers to enjoy disagreeing with me. The book is especially for

- People who are spiritually inquisitive or question major parts of their church's doctrines
- Students seeking fodder for late-night bull sessions
- Fellow dissidents, doubters, heretics, and seekers of truth.
- Nones

Nones, that is, people who are atheists or agnostics or "nothing in particular," reportedly outnumber all Americans except Catholics and Evangelicals. The most common reason that Nones give for not affiliating with a church is the questions they have about traditional religious teachings. Since the book is full of such questions, many Nones may find it helpful.

The book asks many questions and questions many traditional answers. It is not for people who seek certainty or believe they have found it.

An icon of the Virgin Mary in the Eastern Orthodox tradition may seem like an odd choice for the cover of a book that offers unorthodox reflections on Christianity, and perhaps it is. For me, the choice suggests an openness to seeking Truth in all faiths and none, while the icon unites the mother of Jesus with the cosmos that God is still creating. Perhaps Sister Bernadette's "Mary of the Cosmos" will spark some reflections or even heresies of your own.

Malcolm Bell
Randolph Center, Vermont

Introduction

A friendly flame warms hands and heart. Fierce fire destroys. A flickering candle lights our way, and so, if we choose, does faith. In a simpler age, certain church fathers, believing that they could preserve their truths by incinerating contrary ideas, used flame to consume heretics. I hope that my reflections give warmth and stimulate thought, whether or not they seem heretical. Heresies may jar, yet stimulate the search for truth. Which may be heresy to write.

I should say a few words about my faith journey, since it is fair to call it the bias from which I wrote the book. And about the Quaker Way because it underlies much of that bias even though I say little about it except in this introduction. And about the writing itself, which wasn't dashed off but took me more than forty years.

My Faith

When I was thirteen, the teacher of my Sunday school's confirmation class at Brooklyn's Church of the Holy Trinity told us to memorize, among other things, the Apostles' Creed as written in our *Book of Common Prayer*. The last paragraph said:

> I believe in the Holy Ghost; The holy Catholic Church, The Communion of Saints; The Forgiveness of sins: The Resurrection of the body: And the Life everlasting. Amen.

No problem, I thought, with the Holy Ghost, as the Holy Spirit was called back then; but why did we Episcopalians, as I was then, say we believed in the Catholic Church? No problem about the forgiveness of sins because forgiveness is in the Lord's Prayer and sounded like a good idea, but what was The Communion of Saints and what did it have to do with me? The resurrection of people's bodies struck me as bizarre; it still does. Will the corpses arise as real people or simply zombies? Will they eat, bicker, copulate, live forever, die in auto accidents? My spiritual journey began, not with what I memorized, but with what I began to question.

Looking inward, I see two faiths. One comes from what I observe, learn about the physical world, figure out, and imagine. The other comes from the minds and hearts of other people, from Christianity, the ever-challenging Bible, portions of other religions, and works of philosophy and literature. My first faith tests the second. The second informs the first.

I have more faith in God than in any account of God that I know about. I am certain that God created the world and love permeates where we let it. I believe without certainty that we live on beyond our mortal lives. For most matters of faith, the choice is to be certain and often wrong or to seek and maybe err less. I choose the latter. It may be more sound. It's surely more fun.

Profound as the Bible often is, it was the great outdoors and the revelations of science that convinced me that creation is far too miraculous to have happened by chance—and since not by chance, then by a Being that many of us call God. Some years ago, Bill Bryson's popular book *A Short History of Nearly Everything*, followed by other books on scientific subjects, showed me many of the awesome challenges that God overcame in creating the clouds of hydrogen and helium that coalesced into blazing stars, the furnaces of the stars that transformed these gases into the heavier elements, then the enormous amounts of the energy and time it took to fashion a tiny portion of these elements into the incredibly warm, well-watered, intricately functioning planet Earth, and at last in causing life, including you and me, to flourish on it. The God of nature suggests the nature of God.

I'm certain that God created the cosmos, us, and everything else that's in it; I'm pretty sure that God also intervenes in life on Earth, though not as much as many people think and obviously not enough to prevent all tragedies. Jesus was divinely inspired and the soundest teacher I know about. I agree with Pope Paul VI that if you want peace, work for justice, which I take to mean social and economic as well as legal justice.

What I do matters more than what I believe, though the latter informs much of the former. Specifically, I care most about what I do, directly or by giving money, to feed the hungry, clothe the naked, help other needy people, and fix the system that keeps so many people needy in our land of plenty. What I believe about God and Jesus isn't all that important except to the extent that it guides what I do.

The Quaker Way

In 1979, I met the woman for me. Her name is named Nancy, and later that year she became my wife. Since she was a Quaker and by then I belonged to a United Church of Christ, we attended each other's services every other

Sunday; and I soon felt more at home among her people than mine. While reading several books about Quakers, I also found myself agreeing, or already in agreement, with almost all of their faith, values, and ways of living. In due course, I joined the Wilton (CT) Friends Meeting and, by so doing, the Religious Society of Friends.

It was liberating to learn that Quakers are not asked to believe any particular narrative, nothing like the Apostles' Creed or Nicene Creed. We do, though, believe that a divine spark—what Friends call an Inward Light or That of God—burns within each person, even in people who cause great harm. It follows that the bit of God in everyone makes everyone equal to everyone else before God; and it offers guidance to everyone. God's truths exist, not only in a particular faith or book or prophet's teachings, but may spring forth from any person at any time and place, even from you and me. It lives within us all, though we often suppress or ignore it.

Saint Benedict of Nursia, Italy, said in the Sixth Century, "Listen with the ear of your heart and hear the voice of God." For me, the voice of God sends the leadings—the urges to do what's right—of my best self, which I do well to heed. I cannot feel certain that my Inward Light is actually a bit of the Almighty, but I am certain it is my best self, what Abe Lincoln might have called my better angels. I also believe that I do well to question, doubt, and test these leadings. Are they, instead, the seductions of my own bias, ignorance, self-interest, or error? I hear the leadings best during the silence of a Meeting for Worship or in a solitary walk or a quiet talk with Nancy or someone else I trust or a long night's insomnia.

The simplicity—some would call it paucity—of doctrine leaves Quakers with more freedom and fewer moorings than many faithful people seem to feel comfortable with. Such moorings as we have come in good part from our Scripture-based testimonies, which are neither a creed nor words spoken in a court of law but a Quaker term for a set of principles, guidelines, values, priorities.[1] With minor variations among Quakers, they are: simplicity and simple living, peace, integrity, community, the equality of everyone, stewardship of the Earth, and service to others. Quakers, of course, have no monopoly on these values; other faiths profess that a bit of Divinity abides in everyone, and they espouse similar values or principles for how to live.

Rabbi Hillel sounded even less creedal than Quakers when he said in Jesus's day, "What is hateful to you, do not do to your neighbor. That is the whole Torah. The rest is commentary."

Writing the Book

During my first forty or so years, I gave little thought to the direction and purpose of my life and to what I truly wanted to do with the slowly shrinking rest of it. All the same, while I was unmarried during the 1970's, I took several steps towards fulfilling a plan that had long tiptoed through the back of my mind, that is, to go on a solitary retreat for several months with a Bible, several pens, and a fresh pack of legal pads on the rocky island of Iona, which rises out of the waters off the west coast of Scotland. There I'd try to figure things out. My friend-since-high-school Jim Keller had helped to rebuild the ancient abbey on Iona while he was becoming a Presbyterian minister some years earlier; I started, through him, to arrange the particulars for carrying out the plan.

But meeting Nancy scotched the plan, though one sunny day a few years later, she and I visited Iona and the abbey. Perfect as they looked—a gray stone gem set on a green meadow that rose from the chilly, white-capped blue—I never doubted my choice. But my late-blooming urge to think things through was not to be denied; around then I began the years of jotting down my thoughts and questions about life and faith, more than I could possibly have worked out in a few months on that windswept island. Instead of filling a few legal pads during a single summer, I gradually wrote this book.

I am a retired lawyer, and I write as a relatively well-informed layman for other laypeople. While my views are mostly simple, one reason that I dare to venture them is that the views of many eminent theologians strike me as being so encrusted with tradition, received wisdom, and excess logic that they often miss the mark. So many eminent people have gotten so much so wrong during so many centuries that when I err, I am in good company. To the extent that other people agree with my departures from orthodoxy, I suspect that this sometimes speaks less to our sagacity or ignorance than to the shortcomings of orthodoxy. The basics of religion are not arcane, but within the reach of nearly everyone. Why would God reserve faith and truth for a learned few? Wealth may be for one percent of the people; faith is not.

In the Seventeenth Century, the French scientist and philosopher Blaise Pascal wrote a classic defense of Christianity in the form of his *Pensées*, meaning thoughts. While I am neither a scientist nor a philosopher, I have learned many realities about the cosmos that neither Pascal nor the men who wrote the Bible could have known, but that modern astronomers, physicists, biologists, and other scientists have since discovered and students in a decent high school science course are taught. Popular books by atheists like Christopher Hitchens and Richard Dawkins have used these scientific discoveries, often soundly, to expose factual errors in the ancient Scriptures. I use them to illustrate the magnificence of God's creation. It's fine for atheists to disagree with me; I suspect that atheists are part of God's plan.

Mindful of my ignorance, I try not to opine beyond my competence. I assume that all my thoughts have been thought before, though maybe not in these words. I repeat a number of thoughts in several essays, not unduly I hope, because I see value in considering them from more than one perspective. While I call my entries reflections, they may also be called prejudices. A person in Quebec might call them pensées.

Writing them helped to crystallize my own beliefs, and I hope they will help other people to crystallize theirs, whether or not theirs agree with mine. I won't be surprised if many Quakers disagree with much that's here, yet we'll still be Friends. Though a seeker, I do not seek to convince anyone that any of my reflections are sound, if indeed they are. My aim is not to convince or convert but to stimulate.

Many people have been raised to feel guilt when their thoughts diverge from traditional Christian doctrine. I hope, too, that seeing similar thoughts written here may reduce their guilt.

Since the book neither tells a story nor develops an argument, it need not be read from front to back. If you skip ahead, you can't stumble onto a spoiler. There aren't any.

One of the best adventures I had at Harvard College was to read a bunch of plays by George Bernard Shaw, not because they were assigned (they weren't), but because it was so stimulating to disagree with so much of what his characters proclaimed. Doing this often led me to discover what I thought. I hope that you find it as stimulating to disagree with me, to the extent that you do, as I did disagreeing with Shaw. Perhaps you, too, will discover a thing or two about your own thinking.

Unprogrammed Quaker Meetings for Worship are silent except when one or another worshipper utters a brief message. Most of the reflections in this book come in discrete, stand-alone paragraphs, as if they were written versions of the messages that any worshipper might offer. Quakers leave silences between each other's messages; I have left asterisks between mine. The book is, if you will, a collection of Friendly messages bundled by topic.

My time of seeking is nearly through, not because I've found the truth, but because I'm ninety-two. Yet I hope to remain a seeker as long as the flame of life burns within me.

God

A man walks the long trail up the mountain, the brown leaves soft beneath his boots, until he stands, clammy with sweat, on a rock against the gray sky. Knowing he is alone, he prays in a loud voice to his God, his words vanishing in the air. The wind sighs through the green needles of the pines below him as a hawk wheels high above and no one answers. Who sends the wind? Who makes the hawk to fly and the man to trust?

* * *

The hawk spies a brown rabbit leaping across the green of the valley below. He swoops and plunges, talons first, then flaps onto a stump, shreds the furry body with his beak, and gulps the warm flesh down. Who made the rabbit and the hawk? If God created a world in which flesh devours flesh and a rabbit's future may become a hawk's supper, what does this say about life and death and God?

* * *

One of the few things about God that I'm sure of is that God is beyond my comprehension and is hence a Mystery. If God were fully revealed to me, would this still be so? I cannot know. Is there, as Quakers and many others believe, a bit of God within me? Again, I cannot know. I could believe it on faith, but why should I? And what difference does it make whether I call it a bit of God or simply my best self? Either way, it's as God caused or permitted me to evolve. Either way it guides the best of what I do.

* * *

What can one say about the most significant Being there is when that Being is largely unknowable? My own conclusions so far: 1. God created matter, energy, natural forces, and the laws that govern them. 2. Much about God will remain a mystery that no one will penetrate in this lifetime, including the extent, if any, to which God intervenes in mundane matters. 3. However much suffering and early death God may prevent, there is much of them that God does not prevent. 4. Love is a palpable element of God. 5. Godly ways to treat other people usually become clear to those who care to seek them.

* * *

On the day after Christmas in 2009, Brooke Gladstone of National Public Radio told her audience, "May God, or, if you like, random chance, bless us, everyone." Who or what but God or random chance could have created the cosmos and life?

* * *

Chance must be a major tool in God's kit. Questions we cannot answer: when, if ever, does God direct Chance? When does God leave Chance to chance?

* * *

One way that I think God enters the world is through people being their best, most godly selves, helping other people in need, comforting those in sorrow, and trying to make the world a better place. I used to find it pretentious to think that mere humans can act as "hands of God." Now I believe it. As the saying goes, If not us, who? If not now, when?

* * *

The more components of Creation that had a very slim chance of happening, yet did happen, the more likely it is that God, rather than Chance, caused them to happen. Did the marvels of photosynthesis happen by chance? The versatility of carbon, which makes us possible? And the vast energy stored in matter ($e = mc2$, energy equals mass times the velocity of light—186,000 miles per second—squared), which makes it possible for stars like the Sun to burn fiercely for billions of years without consuming themselves, while single cells took their sweet time evolving into us?

* * *

Scientists might, if they cared to, use their knowledge and methodology to calculate what the odds are against all the long shots that were needed to give us the relatively advanced life that we enjoy on relatively gentle Earth spinning through the vast, frigid, violent void. The greater the number of very slim chances and apparently lucky breaks, then the clearer it becomes that we are perceiving God's work. The belief that we see God through Nature has been around for centuries if not millennia, yet only through today's scientific discoveries can we glimpse the multitude, magnitude, and complexities of the essential contributions to our existence that combine to give the lie to the claim that all of them happened by chance. The odds that Chance alone created life as we know it look slimmer than the odds against drawing successfully to an inside straight a thousand straight times—or of a monkey and its progeny eventually typing out *Moby Dick*. And even if this line of lucky simians somehow succeeded in writing that great novel, we might look for the hidden hand of a Herman Melville.

* * *

Those who seek proof that God exists tend to demand the absolute proof that mathematicians require for their theories. But I was a lawyer. Proof beyond a reasonable doubt and to a moral certainty—that is, less than 100% but pretty damn certain—is the highest standard that we lawyers demand or expect.

If I were trying to prove the case that God the Creator exists and creates, I would first call top scientists to the witness stand and ask them to explain the host of interdependent circumstances upon which our being here today depended, for example, that stars created the heavy elements that coalesced into planets; planets swing around stars; Earth is a warm distance from the Sun; a single moon is of a size and at a distance to serve the Earth as it does; water and carbon have their amazing properties; DNA has the properties it needs to do the jobs it does; and on and on. Then I'd call the top gamblers of the world to the stand and ask them the odds that by chance alone all these circumstances would occur in the sequences and combinations that were essential to giving us the Creation we've got, and us the ability to talk about it.

* * *

Would it make us better people if someone proves God's existence to a mathematical certainty? Or only more anxious and less free?

* * *

"Our responding to life's unfairness with sympathy and with righteous indignation, God's compassion and God's anger working through us, may be the surest proof of all of God's reality."

—Rabbi Harold S. Kushner[2]

* * *

For my friend since high school Don Conover, at least three realities assure us of the reality of God: the laws of nature that govern our world and all its creatures; our moral awareness that doing what's right matters more than being selfish; and the joy we take in being alive, in romantic love, and in the beauties of nature, art, and all else we find beautiful.

* * *

Paradoxically, it's our God-given sense of justice and fairness that tempts us to doubt that God exists when we perceive that we are suffering unfairly or unjustly.

* * *

It seems paradoxical but true that God remains mysterious yet gives peace and comfort to those who turn to God.

* * *

Also paradoxical: Mysterious as God remains, God is at the heart of all reality.

* * *

People who die and come back—that is, have near-death experiences—say that they felt enveloped by love. Perhaps they were enveloped by God.

* * *

I grow weary when people assure us in tones of authority that God thinks this or that. Faithful as I believe they are trying to be, all they are telling us is what they think God thinks.

* * *

In what language, if any, does God think? Does God think at all, as we understand the term, or proceed in another way?

* * *

Since God has chosen to be mysterious, why should God be angry or upset if someone doesn't get it right about God? Many people take the heresies they perceive in others too seriously, especially since they themselves inevitably err.

* * *

I grew up attending the Church of the Holy Trinity. Many churches bear that name. In those days, Trinity meant God the Father, God the Son, and God the Holy Ghost. Today *Father* may be *Creator*, and *Holy Ghost* has been renamed *Holy Spirit*. Beyond believing Jesus to have been the most godly person I know about, I do not consider him to be an aspect of God, and surely not co-eternal with God: Jesus existed before beginning of the cosmos 13.8 billion years ago? Did God choose to beget a son billions of years before the likes of humans evolved on any planet? Likewise, while I believe we know enough about God to call God the *Creator*, I don't see that we know enough to separate God into Creator and Spirit. What would such a separation mean, and why would it matter? Is it only the Spirit that intervenes today? Muslims and Jews believe in one God; and the one God is mysterious enough for me, without adding a mystery that strikes me as being as unsolvable as the sound of one hand clapping. My own supposition is that the Holy Spirit is an *aspect* of the one God, one among many aspects known and unknown. If, as I believe, the Holy Spirit suffused the man Jesus, he became a vehicle for the one God.

* * *

It seems inaccurate to attribute one sex or the other to God. If there is one God, there is presumably no other god to mate with and no procreating of more gods.

* * *

I am fairly sure that God is neither *He* nor *She*; and calling God *It* sounds impersonal or even inanimate. While referring to God as *She* may have served as a temporary fix for the millennia of calling God *He*, *She* is as sexist and dismissible as *He* is.[i] Lacking an adequate pronoun for God, I repeat the noun.

* * *

Another reason for not assigning a gender to God: If God were he or she, God would presumably not be complete, but would instead be missing a complementary part. Men tend to have some virtues that women don't, women tend to have some virtues that men don't, and *vive la différence*; but it's nice to think that God has them all.

* * *

As long as we call God Father, can women ever enjoy full equality with men?

* * *

Many feminists insist on calling God *She* but seem satisfied to let the Devil be *he*.

* * *

God sits on a throne? Presumably God has neither a need to sit nor a butt to sit upon.

* * *

Robert Wright, author of *The Evolution of God:*[3] • "The test of a conception of God is, What kind of a person does it turn you into?" • "Love and truth may be manifestations of divinity, and the more we manifest them, the closer we come to being godly." • "Immature faith is thinking we are more special to God than other people are."

* * *

I am told and tend to believe that action reveals character. All that our sens-

---

i People who use plural pronouns such as "they" to stand for singular subjects such as "anyone" might logically use "they" to refer to the one God—a grammatical error that suggests polytheism.

es and sciences tell us about Creation suggest, in human terms, the Creator's vast intelligence, power, and longevity.

* * *

Yes, as we know people by their deeds and they know us by ours, we know something about God from God's Creation and perhaps God's other deeds. But we also know that our deeds tell only part of who we are, and so it must be with God. However much we infer from God's handiwork, the Mystery remains.

* * *

Is God all-powerful? All we can know for sure is that God had the power to create all this, presumably from nothing. While it's hard to imagine that God has always existed, it strikes me as the most probable possibility.

* * *

We cannot begin to glimpse the intelligence and power of God until we begin to understand the vastness of space, the complexity of matter, and ingenuity of life's processes and adaptations.

* * *

At Matthew 22:37-38, Jesus said, "'You shall love the Lord your God with all your heart, and with all your soul, and with all your mind.' This is the greatest and first commandment." (NRSV) Mark 12:30 and Luke 10:27 are similar. In the first place, I don't believe that true feeling can be felt on command. Second, while I feel tremendous admiration and gratitude for God, I find it very hard to feel love for a Mystery, or even for a man who manifested that Mystery in a distant time and culture.

* * *

The USA, being for now the mightiest nation on a tiny planet in the vast sweep of time and space, is called a superpower. No, the only *superpower* is the Almighty.

* * *

If God is as ubiquitous as we are told, then God is present not only on tiny Earth but also across billions of light years throughout all Creation and particularly on every planet. The Kepler space telescope, which was aloft for more than nine years ending in 2018, discovered sufficient evidence for scientists to conclude that there are more planets than stars in our galaxy, and that about ten billion of these planets are sufficiently warm, watered, and otherwise endowed to be habitable by life as we know it.[4] And bear in mind that ours is only one out of billions of galaxies. So there must be millions or billions of planets that have life that's intelligent. I see no reason why God would not be there for those beings as God is here for us.

* * *

The modestly improving chances of our finding another scientifically advanced civilization in our own Milky Way galaxy are commonly calculated by considering the Drake Equation,[ii] which was worked out in 1961 by astronomer Frank Drake, who was a pioneer in the search for extra-terrestrial intelligent life, a.k.a., SETI. The Drake Equation may yield a number that satisfies atheists; but for me that number is far too low because it omits a factor that greatly increases the number of such planets, namely, that God exists and favors life. God's evident desire to create intelligent life on Earth suggests that God may well have arranged for such life to appear on far more planets than the probability-based (chance-based) Drake Equation would predict. According to a 2020 analysis of Kepler data, there are probably around 300 million planets at a "Goldilocks" distance (i.e., not too hot or cold to have water) in the Milky Way galaxy alone. For if God created many millions of Earth-like planets in the Milky Way alone, and God created life on Earth, why would God leave all those other planets devoid of life?

* * *

Though it's easy to say that God is everywhere, I find it next to impossible to imagine any Being being everywhere. Though if life exists in all things, then perhaps God does too.

* * *

The Bible's boast that God made people in God's image may contain a grain of truth—what Quakers call That of God within each of us. But consider that much of humankind seeks power, possessions, and glory by fair means and foul; many people are petty, nasty, dishonest, and could not care less about their fellows or are outright cruel. I suppose the boast that we are in God's image is not meant to mean that God has the flaw that we have.

* * *

---

ii According to Drake's equation, these chances are equal to the product of: the rate of formation of suitable stars, times the fraction of these stars that have planets orbiting them, times the number of such planets with a suitable environment (for example, that are in the "Goldilocks" range), times the fraction of such planets on which life appears, times the fraction of those planets on which that life becomes intelligent, times the fraction of those planets on which that intelligent life advances enough to send signals into space (as we currently send out radio signals), times the period of time during which those civilizations send out those signals. As explained by Dennis Overbye in the Nov. 5, 2013, *New York Times*. Incidentally, Frank Drake was once married to my first cousin, composer Elizabeth Bell (Elizabeth Bell Drake Friou).

Surely conscious life is a condition that we and many other creatures share with God. Beyond that, is life itself an element of God? An inexhaustible element? Is there That of God, a tiny portion of God, in every creature, even the lowliest cockroach and corona virus? If so, when God gives life to all such creatures, God is giving bit of God's self, and the life of every such creature is even more sacred than most of us commonly realize. But not so sacred, I suppose, that carnivores and omnivores should not kill in order to live. Or that I won't slap a mosquito. But consider the vast sacrilege of war, the willful smashing of God's living temples.

※ ※ ※

God created us, fair enough. In response, we created a God of Our Adjectives. It strikes me as presumptuous to attribute human qualities, no matter how exalted or flattering, to God. *Omnipotent, omniscient, benevolent,* and *ubiquitous* constitute futile efforts, however well meant, to reduce God to human terms and imprison God within our puny ability to comprehend.

※ ※ ※

Though God is largely incomprehensible, many people presume to describe and thereby confine God in a gilded cage of lofty adjectives like *omnipotent, omniscient, benevolent,* and *perfect.* Thus we confound ourselves and may lose our faith when we fail to understand how this God of our creation lets bad things befall good people as readily as hapless rabbits. I feel that God loves us, though not, I suppose, as one person may love another. How could the God that created this miraculous Earth and gave us life upon it not love us?

※ ※ ※

Through the ages people have understandably attributed to God the highest virtues they could conceive of. Thus they created God in an image that probably expressed their awe, unwilling to acknowledge that God's nature is beyond their puny ability to comprehend, and that humans' notions of these virtues may apply to God only randomly if at all.

※ ※ ※

Bestowing human attributes upon God hinders people's efforts to appreciate what God is and does. When we think about God, I suggest we'd come closer to the mark if we try to put ourselves very humbly into God's shoes to the extent of imagining the enormous challenges that God overcame in order to make everything in the cosmos work as exquisitely (albeit, in the judgment of many, imperfectly) as it does, while remaining far enough behind the curtain that God's existence cannot be proved absolutely and people who don't want to believe in the Creator of everything don't have to.

* * *

The contemporary philosopher of religion Richard Swinburne follows the tradition of finding evidence of God in the wonders of Nature as increasingly revealed by science; but he also follows the tradition of assigning humanly conceived attributes to God, writing that God has "infinite power… infinite knowledge… and infinite freedom" … except that, "being perfectly good," God does not have "the freedom to choose between good and evil."[5] Really? By allowing bad things to happen to good people, isn't God choosing what we call *evil*? Or does God lack, not the will, but the power to stop these bad things? The glorious attributes that many humans assign to God prompt one to answer yes, but answering yes is unnecessary and unfair to God. This quandary can be avoided by recognizing that these well-intended attributes do not fetter God. I'd like to think that in God's grand scheme, even the worst evils that God seems to allow people to do are, in fact, either the lesser of two evils or preferable to intervening in an obvious way or else worse than God foresaw we'd do when God gave us freedom. Even the Holocaust?

* * *

The Holocaust may or may not have tested God. It certainly tested many people's conceptions of God and faith in God.

* * *

We place unrealistic expectations on God, and many of us grow angry with God when God does not fulfill them. We know of the Holocaust that God did not prevent, but not of the holocausts that God may have prevented.

* * *

It is unfair to God to expect God to conform to our standards of goodness, power, and occasions for divine intervention, and then to fault God or stop believing in God when we suppose that God has not obeyed our priorities. After Copernicus made the case that the planets orbit the Sun, a good number of people believed that the orbits were perfect circles because, they were certain, God would not create an imperfect solar system. Then Johannes Kepler proved that the orbits are not circles but ellipses that have the Sun as one of their foci. The notion that a perfect God would have presented us with a perfect Creation, as we define *perfect*, strikes me as being presumptuous and wrong. How many perfect people did God create? We don't get to define or impose *perfect* on God — or, if we're sensible, on our children.

* * *

It seems presumptuous to conclude that God does not exist because we perceive that God has not measured up to our standards; or to say that if God existed, God would have made what we consider a more efficient world or human body as we define *efficient*. The Scottish philosopher David Hume argued that since we improve on Nature, how could an all-powerful God have created anything as imperfect as Nature? But that's *improve on* by our standards; it assumes that God wanted to meet our standards of excellence, efficiency, and so on from the get-go. Isn't God allowed to value God's own process of evolution more highly than an instantly created "perfect" human body that would satisfy David Hume, whose own body was fat?

* * *

The fact that we can only speculate about why we exist should, I think, deter us from presuming to describe God by lofty adjectives. But can we at least say that God loves us? I think so, for God gave us the magnificent gift of life upon this miraculously benign speck of the cosmos that God so magnificently created.

* * *

I suspect that God is pleased when people use these adjectives, inaccurate as they may be, because they show that the people who use them mean God well.

* * *

To have created us in the fully developed form that Adam is said to have had would have showed God's hand rather obviously, which is obviously not what God wanted.

* * *

I believe that God loves you, whoever you are, and me as much as God loves anyone else, loves Conservatives and Liberals equally, loves the Other as much as the Us. This is a part of what equality means—however radical or threatening or unthinkable an idea this may be.

* * *

The Being that we call the God of love is also the God of the food chain, the earthquake, the mosquito, dementia, and the survival of the fittest. Loving that God means loving the Creator of vipers, typhoons, AIDS, cancer, Covid-19, and cockroaches.

* * *

"Would the world ever have been made if its maker had been afraid of making trouble? Making life means making trouble."

—George Bernard Shaw[6]

* * *

Survival of the fittest means the early deaths of the less fit and the unlucky. In addition, there have been at least five mass extinctions in the last five hundred million years, in which fifty to ninety percent of all *species* died off. Was there a way to create the higher animals, including us, that would look less cruel from a human perspective? What kinder way do you suggest? The account in Genesis? Did God choose evolution and the extinctions, with all the suffering and early death that they entailed? Or not?

* * *

I look from my window at the silent forest dark under a starry sky. The silence occasionally breaks as one of God's creatures makes its supper out of another of God's creatures.

* * *

Isaiah 11:6 tells us, "The wolf also shall dwell with the lamb, and the leopard shall lie down with the kid...and a little child shall lead them." But if the wolf doesn't eat the lamb and the leopard doesn't eat the kid, or some equivalent meat, they will soon starve. This reality may look cruel, as does the reality that zillions of less fit members of various species die young while the fittest adapt and evolve. Yet the loving and intelligent God is, for me, also a God of life; and for life to flourish, so, it seems, must death.

We have long understood that it's necessary and sad but not cruel for old flora and fauna (including us) to die in order to make room for the next and so on; and it also seems necessary for many animals to die young for the balance of nature to thrive—as a short, excellent *National Geographics* film about the benefits arising from the return of wolves to Yellowstone National Park[7] well illustrates—and for so many new and diverse species to flourish over much of the Earth. On balance, life has been winning for eons and is winning now, except as human greed and shortsightedness assault Nature.

* * *

Who is to say that God does not value the so-called lower animals? Is there any reason to doubt that God loves all life, both life that feeds on other life and life that is fed upon?

* * *

If the spark of life may be a spark of God within us, then is this also so in so-called lower animals? I think so.

* * *

How could a loving God let us die of a loathsome disease? A hard question, but consider the alternative, that is, what life would be like if, in order to assure our comfort and prolong our earthly existence, God regularly broke the laws by which God organized the intricate cosmos. As Jesus is said to have broken them. How old was Lazarus when he died again after Jesus is said to have revived him? What caused his second death? Does God have the power to break the laws of Nature that God created? I believe so, though many don't. Did God grant that power to a man whom God wished to elevate in people's eyes? So we are told, and are told that Jesus passed that power on to some of his followers. Really? Why would God or Jesus have done that?

* * *

Does God have feelings that are more or less like ours? If so, what does God feel when bad things happen to good people? When people destroy other people in wars, gang fights, or the Holocaust? When so many torture so many, and when Roman soldiers, obeying orders, nailed Jesus to a cross? We humans often pay a steep price for our gift of free will—a gift apparently not bestowed on ants. The occasions when God does not intervene to prevent harm, great or small, to humans do not mean that their suffering does not pain God as well. Rather, I suspect that God, too, pays a price for the free will that God gives us, and that people who hurt other people thereby hurt, or at least disappoint, God.

* * *

I suspect, too, that if God intervenes at all in people's affairs, it's not nearly as much as many people believe. The evil that people do—that is, the harm that people cause—results from people's choices or their indifference, not God's. God may be responsible for people-made horrors only to the extent that God chose to create us through an evolution that included the survival of the most wily and aggressive, while many of our harmful choices result from our being incompletely evolved even now. Yet who is wise or bold enough to say how God should have created us other than by this often brutal evolution? The accounts in Genesis 1 and 2 are fetching stories but not what actually happened.

* * *

Consider the Holocaust, all the wars and ethnic cleansings, climate change, the world's currently unused stocks of biological and nuclear weapons, and so on. It may be consoling to suppose that though we humans may choose to self-destruct, more humble and compassionate beings are likely to be carrying on on other planets; and that if a Jesus-like figure came among them, they probably heeded him or her on some of those planets more sensibly than we have done on ours. If it's not too late to rescue life on Earth, it soon may be. Some scientists believe that the sixth mass extinction is in progress, and obviously some idiot or accident may touch off a nuclear war. As God would apparently have it, it was or still is up to us.

* * *

"Though I walk through the valley of the shadow of death, I will fear no evil for thou art with me. Thy rod and thy staff, they comfort me...." (Psalm 23) Sooner or later, the notion that God stops harm from befalling us is off-putting because harm does befall us. (Though we shan't know for sure whether God ever saves us from harm, surviving a near miss may cause us to suspect it.) Having God with us when harm threatens may not block the harm, but it may sustain us through it when we let it. God sustaining us can be a comforting idea, once we accept life's realities, and it's also believable because we can, if we wish, feel it happening.

* * *

Perhaps God's grace is to grant us peace when we follow God's ways.

* * *

The peace of God is everyone's for the taking.

* * *

If God always took care of us, wouldn't we wither?

* * *

Righteous people sometimes teach us a false God, one who always saves good people from harm. Psalm 121 says, "The sun shall not smite thee by day nor the moon by night." Tell that to people with sunstroke or melanoma. But in Psalm 23, "Thy rod and thy staff, they comfort me." Those implements are said, not to protect or save me, but to *comfort* me. They signify that God is with me if I am with God. Though they look like weapons that God could use to defend me, that's not to be counted on. God's comfort is.

* * *

My God is a God of life. Life flourishes with amazing vigor and in amazing places. Even when life is taken, it is often in the interest of life. Consider carnivores and us omnivores, and the soldiers and firefighters and ants that sacrifice their lives for their fellows.

* * *

We are told that God is a God of love, yet God's love may be hard to discern when things go terribly wrong. This is true even if we believe that God does not micromanage the lives of the seven billion or so souls on Earth—and God knows how many other souls on distant planets. Beyond question, it seems, God *is* a God of life though death is an inevitable part of life.

* * *

I cannot believe that God micromanages the lives of each of those seven billion or so souls, that is, that we are all God's wind-up toys. Are we no more miraculous than the ant? What would our reason for being be if God totally managed us? Simply to serve as a step in the evolution of a form of life that will be "higher" than us and maybe truly free? Don't we think for ourselves on many matters, even if it's not as many as we may suppose?

* * *

Even if we assume that God has the power to micromanage the lives of billions of people, I don't see why God would choose to do that, to rule out our free will and direct us to choose certain jobs or trips or spouses, to bestow certain joys and inflict certain suffering on us, and so on. We may not know why we are here, but it cannot be to be God's wind-up toys.

* * *

I suppose that the God out there does not direct the course of our lives— does not decide that I'll be a doctor or a ditch digger and so forth. Rather, we make these decisions ourselves or let parents or events or glands or other mundane forces make them for us. To the extent that the best or most godly part of ourselves makes them, that may be how God guides us by way of our free will.

* * *

Suppose that God is all powerful in creating and breaking the rules that govern life on Earth, but judges it best to preserve these rules even at the cost of much human pain and suffering—and, given the way we are now headed, perhaps extinction.

* * *

Suppose, again, that God is omnipotent but chooses not to violate the laws of Nature that God created, except maybe here and there where God's hand won't show. And suppose the greater good is for people not to perceive God as breaking these laws. Sometimes, I suspect, salutary coincidences come from the God behind the curtain.

* * *

It is said that all things work together for good for those who love the Lord. Not quite, I think, but sometimes and perhaps often. While I doubt that God intervenes to the extent of micromanaging us, it seems evident that when we let or invite the force of love (God) into our lives, good things often ensue. I suspect that this is one of God's ways.

* * *

Was it mere happenstance that Lincoln was the President who could and did keep the U.S. together and end slavery during Civil War? Or that Churchill may have been the only Prime Minister who could have led Britain to hold out against Hitler in 1940-1941? Or that Werner Heisenberg, the brilliant German scientist who was in a position to give Hitler the atomic bomb and with it a terrible victory in World War II, did not do so?[iii] Or that John Kennedy, and not a more hawkish person, was President during the 1962 Cuban Missile Crisis when any rash act could have touched off a nuclear war?

* * *

Note that I have ventured to offer quite a bit about God the Creator, less about God the Intervenor, and little or no proof of the latter except anecdotes and a general feeling. Does God intervene only through the powers of love and peace and people acting as hands of God, or more directly too? Again, I feel it's the latter. It is far easier to believe in God the Creator than in God the Intervenor—as I suspect God would have it. Were it otherwise, free will would be compromised and only fools would sin.

* * *

My friend Don Conover said that God's "ultimate intervention was to send Jesus to earth to make plain what the good life should be.... [H]is intervention through Jesus's lessons for how we should behave is at the core of Christianity."

* * *

I suppose that God sees into what we call the future. Some people, too, report having had amazing foreknowledge of future events. Consider the soldier with an injury, I believe, to his head during World War I who "hallucinated" that the church he was in in France was being struck by a Ger-

---

iii Heisenberg's reasons for denying Hitler the Bomb and the victory remain unclear. Was it his conscience or merely an uncharacteristic lapse of his intellect? The question is discussed brilliantly in Michael Frayn's play *Copenhagen* and his postscript to the play, and comprehensively by Thomas Powers in *Heisenberg's War: The Secret History of The German Bomb* (Da Capo Press, 2000).

man shell; he got himself and his companion outside before a shell actually struck the church killing many inside. Consider, too, the warning that Peter Hurkos, a Dutchman, gave to a friend of his during World War II not to meet X at Y corner at Z time of day because if he did, the Nazis would take him—as the friend did and the Nazis did. Now and then my wife Nancy has a strong sense of what is going to happen, and it does. Then there was the wife of a newspaper obituary writer who would often tell him to go to his file and update so-and-so's draft obit shortly before that person (who was not known to be ill) died. I'm sure that many people have heard such whisperings of foreknowledge. If some people can glimpse the future now and then, I expect that God can see it always. If so, God foresaw the Holocaust, yet let it happen. Does that make God evil? Or seriously dedicated to leaving much or all of our future up to us? Or merely inscrutable? We always knew that God was inscrutable.

* * *

What about Sister Dianna Ortiz? At the age of six, she told her family that she would become a nun; and growing up in Grants, New Mexico, she developed a special feeling for the downtrodden Native Americans who lived there. She came east to Brescia College; upon graduating, she joined the Order of St. Ursula and began a useful and comfortable ministry of teaching little children in Kentucky. But a feeling grew within her that God was calling her to teach Native American (specifically, Mayan) children in Guatemala, which she knew was in the throes of a brutal military repression. So there she went, in her late twenties in 1987, to join two experienced and politically savvy nuns in the beautiful green western highlands, in an area where the U.S.-backed army had been freely murdering civilian "suspects." For reasons undisclosed, the security forces singled out Dianna, the naïve neophyte, for death threats. Though terrified, she refused to leave her ministry to these imperiled youngsters.

On November 2, 1989, three members of the CIA-advised secret police kidnapped her, burned her with cigarettes more than one hundred times, gang-raped her, and put her through other hellacious tortures that shattered her being. But she rose up from her ruin to seek justice for herself and for the people of Guatemala, showing a courage and determination that gave inspiration and hope to millions of those oppressed people. Here in the United States, she led other survivors of torture in speaking out—with the unique authority that their trauma bestowed on them—against this abominable and relatively inefficient practice.[8]

Their efforts became even more necessary after the attack of 9/11/2001 moved our government to torture thousands of suspects, some to death, in inept attempts to keep Americans safe. And so Sister Dianna, prominent among many like-minded activists, helped to turn a fragile consensus of U.S. public opinion against this barbaric practice; and the next President acted to end the practice, though his successor favored restoring it.

Did Sister Dianna's self-sacrifice result from the godliness within her, or a choice by an external God, or both? Did God, knowing what would befall her, call her to undergo physical agony and the psychic devastation in 1989 that marked her to the end of her life in 2021, in order to benefit millions of people? Would a good God do that? Consider the fatal torture that God probably knew would befall Jesus yet did not prevent. Or was it that the God who did not intervene to prevent the Holocaust also did not prevent the horror that certain men chose to inflict on this gentle nun; and that she, who had chosen to become a missionary in a danger zone, then chose to become even more a hand of God on Earth? Or did it just work out that way?

* * *

Can Nancy and I, who considered Dianna a friend but can only imagine her pain, still believe that there is That of God within her torturers and their superiors? Yes, though it was damn well hidden when they violated both her body and any bit of decency within themselves.

* * *

Should God intervene to stop people, answering the godliness within themselves, from serving as God's hands if/when God knows that evil people may/will torture/kill them for doing so? I think not. Perhaps God so loves the world that God has sent/inspired many daughters and sons to risk/suffer the sacrifice of themselves to make the world a better place. Or invested these saintly people with so much godliness that they chose of their own free will to risk/incur suffering in order to make it a better place. Echoing, I think, the will of God.

* * *

We people constantly make demands on God, through our prayers and expectations and definitions. In contrast, what does the Lord require of us "but to do justly, and to love mercy, and to walk humbly with thy God?" (Micah 6:8.)

* * *

God gave us life and the Earth to live it on and so much more. What do we give God?

* * *

If we want proof that God loves us, consider the life God gives and the peace God offers.

* * *

One more adjective: Is God eternal? Maybe it's my conceptual limitations, but I cannot conceive how God could have come into being—spontaneously combusted, popped up—out of nothing and nowhere. While the lofty adjectives may, at best, merely approximate a part of the reality of God, I have to believe that the cosmos could not have come into being if God were not enormously powerful and intelligent and eternal.

* * *

Nancy: "I don't see how God could have had a beginning."

* * *

Since you and I and the Earth and the cosmos are, God has always been.

Creation

One day a carpenter named Chance decided to build a house, so he bought an empty lot, assembled the tools and materials he needed, and went to work. Not being very skillful, he proceeded by trial and error and made many mistakes. But being a persistent fellow and having all the time in the world, he eventually created a pretty fair house complete with wiring and plumbing. All by himself.

But who forged the tools, milled the lumber, and produced the insulated copper wire, the pipes, the sinks, and the porcelain toilets? Who created the iron and steel that were malleable enough to be shaped into tools yet hard enough to keep their shapes, and the wood that was soft enough to saw yet strong enough to hold up the house? Who enabled copper wire to carry electricity, and, for that matter, who created copper and electricity? Same questions about the heating, the plumbing, the water that flows through it, and the earth that the house stands upon.

Yes, Chance made the house, but how much help did he receive, and from whom did he receive it? Could all his help have come from other Chances, or are the chances that all these Chances came serendipitously together too improbable to believe?

We know that, given enough time and trials and errors, Chance could possibly have designed and constructed the house—out of all the right stuff that was somehow made available to him. But for all we know, an Architect may have stopped by every now and then to give Chance some guidance and perhaps even lend a hand. Indeed, perhaps it was the Architect who actually decided to build the house; and since he, too, had all the time in the world, he employed Chance to do the job under his supervision. And left us free to conclude, if we wished, that Chance created the house all by himself.

* * *

Regarding Brooke Gladstone's Boxing Day blessing (see p. 2), "May God, or, if you like, random chance bless us, everyone," I think she exhausted the possibilities. Why is there something and not nothing? Because of God or random chance or what else can you plausibly suggest? Could random chance have created all this? Or called the elements into being?

* * *

There are more planets on the loose, hurtling cold and dark through the cosmos, unmoored to any star, than there are planets that orbit stars. We may thank our lucky stars that we orbit one of them at a Goldilocks distance—not too hot or cold. Or maybe thank God.

* * *

The miracle of Creation is a serendipitous mosaic of lesser miracles.

* * *

The Big Bang theory: Everything came from nearly nothing in an instant? Or even in a relatively few eons? I cannot believe a theory that claims (if I understand it correctly) that all the billions of galaxies, the dark matter, black holes, and so on across the cosmos originated in the explosion of a very small mass in a very brief time. Where did this mighty pea come from? In what place and state and time, if any, did it linger before exploding? Was it somehow a self-generating fount of matter and anti-matter? What set it off? If the void is not infinite, what, if anything, lies beyond it? If the Big Bang theory is close to correct, it may correspond to the fabled moment in Genesis when God said, "Let there be light," in one language or another.

* * *

Did God create matter and/or energy before the Big Bang or whatever it was that apparently constituted Step One in God's creation of the current cosmos? Did time exist before this cosmos, or did God create time directly, or is time an inherent component of the cosmos that God created?

* * *

It boggles the mind that after the Big Bang (or whatever it was), the only elements were great quantities of hydrogen plus helium that was 23% as plentiful as hydrogen, and small amounts of deuterium (an isotope of hydrogen) and lithium; that ALL heavier elements were fabricated from these gasses inside the furnaces of the stars and the explosions that blew them apart; and that chunks of all this shrapnel fell together and coalesced into the billions of planets that orbit the Sun and other stars. Our Sun, incidentally, is said to be too small to create elements heavier than iron when it blows—as it will.

* * *

How amazing that gravity causes various gases and miscellaneous other matter in space to coalesce into increasingly large and eventually spherical masses until their weight and internal gravity are so great that they ignite into fusion infernos that burn for billions of years as stars, about which planets wheel and receive sufficient heat and light across many millions of miles of coldest space to make life on Earth and many other planets possible. What gave gravity the property of behaving like this? What gave those atoms the ability to ignite like that? The more that one branch or another of science tells us about the ways the cosmos and it many parts work, the more readily we may admire and praise God for God's creative genius and power.

* * *

Concerning the enormous energy packed into relatively tiny amounts of matter, for which Einstein's equation is e = mc2: Whose bright idea was it to compress energy into matter and turn matter into energy? How did God give hydrogen the potential that enabled the violence of stars that are comprised of this simple element to transform it into the heavier elements that are essential to forming rocky planets like Earth with life like us upon them? Same questions re the facts that huge stars whose burning hydrogen creates and eventually scatters these heavier elements into space burn out in only a hundred million or so years; whereas the nuclear fusion in moderate-size stars like our Sun radiates heat and light in all directions for the billions of years it took for intelligent life to form and flourish on Earth and quite likely on many similar planets? Or that only rare events like the collision of two super-dense neutron stars will produce rare elements like gold and platinum? Back when most of existence was hydrogen atoms whizzing around in a frigid void, who would have thought that intelligent beings would reach such pinnacles of Creation as WalMart and McDonald's?

* * *

Johannes Kepler's second law—which observes that an imaginary line joining any planet to the Sun sweeps out the same area of space as a similar line from any other planet in an equal period of time—provides a further suggestion about the mind (if we can call it that) of God. So does the velocity with which objects whiz through space, smashing and shaking things up, initiating change, and so on. The planets hold their orbits as the Sun's gravity counters the centrifugal force that their velocity around it generates; a particular balance of such gravity and force keeps the Earth in its present benign range of distances from the Sun. Our one big moon lifts and drops the cleansing tides and performs other wonders that aid life on Earth. The ancient devastation from an asteroid's impact off the Yucatan Peninsula of Mexico is said to have wiped huge carnivorous reptiles off the Earth (the fifth mass extinction), thus allowing smaller mammals and eventually us to survive, evolve, and flourish. On the micro side, how did tiny particles and the forces that hold them together in the mostly empty units called atoms get arranged with the characteristics that permit them to combine into all the elements and every material we know about? Consider the miracle of hydrogen, the ultimate source, one proton and one electron. How did the atoms of most elements come to exist with the ability to bind together with the atoms of other elements so as to create compounds that are entirely different from either component, such as oxygen binding with hydrogen to form water, without which there would be no life as we know it? Who endowed atoms and gravity and genes and evolution with the capacities to function as they do? If by any chance it was Chance, who created Chance?

* * *

While I believe that Chance alone cannot have done all this, Chance was most probably one of the tools with which God did it.

* * *

Note God's scatter-shot approach, the abundance that is a part of the ways in which God employs Chance: There are zillions of stars, reportedly some 400 billion in our Milky Way galaxy alone, and more planets than stars. Of the zillions of planets, a relatively small proportion, apparently, can sustain life as we know it. Zillions of tadpoles to produce one frog. Numberless seeds, one plant, one tree. Each man's ejaculation launches zillions of sperms for each one that merges with a woman's waiting ovum to start their evolution into a hungry little baby. For many are called, but few chosen. Matthew 22:14.

* * *

We cannot begin to grasp the intelligence and power of God until we begin to understand the nature and complexity of Creation: the vastness of space as science has described it so far, the hugeness and minuteness of matter, the ways things work, the zillion forms of life, and the interwoven simplicities and complexities of it all.

* * *

A God that had the power to create all that exists probably has the power to do all the things I can imagine that aren't mutually exclusive, plus an enormous number of things beyond my imagining.

* * *

So far as we know, various laws of physics prevail throughout the cosmos. If there were no God, one would expect, not these laws of physics, but the anarchy of chaos.

* * *

Why does so much about Nature have an underlying mathematical beauty?

* * *

As noted above, scattered around the billions of solar systems within the billions of galaxies, there must be very many planets like Earth that have spawned intelligent, capable life. Indeed, it would seem naïve and presumptuous to suppose that only on planet Earth could such life flower. Most likely, intelligent beings, perhaps with bodies similar to ours, live on other planets, though distances are such that we aren't to likely meet any of them during this life, at least not through space travel. We and they likely share some common humanity. Likely too, at least a good portion of them have That of God within them and have produced the likes of Jesus, Mohammed, Buddha, et al. to lead them, as best they can, towards peace and compassion.

* * *

The most intelligent species on many of those planets must, like us, have achieved an ability to destroy all life that dwells there. Probably some of them manage to avoid this peril and some don't. How intelligent were the latter? Which shall we be?

* * *

The creation of life by itself, though miraculous, would not have been sufficient. There had to be a double miracle, first, to light the spark of life, and second, to enable the bearer of life's tiny flame to replicate itself before it died. Were it not for the second miracle, life would simply have been a candle that burned down to darkness. Moreover, exact replications would, over time, be as fatal as no replications. For beings that stayed exactly the same would not mutate nor evolve to adapt to changing conditions. For them, too, darkness would descend.

* * *

The creation scenario that I accept can be called "intelligent design," though not as Evangelicals use that term or as Genesis describes it. One tool of God's design is evolution. But before that, came God's creation of the host of conditions necessary to form a hospitable habitat in which evolution could occur—like the venue, forces, and stuff that Chance needed to build the house I imagined at the beginning of this chapter.

* * *

God the Creator created the food chain: Most creatures can and regularly do serve as supper for other creatures in the balance of Nature and economy of Life.

* * *

The preciousness of life has had its limits. Consider how many lives have been sacrificed in order to move evolution forward. Survival of the fittest is the sunny side of evolution's coin; the dark side is the early deaths of the less fit and the extinction of their kind. Survival is either of the fittest members of a species or else of such mutants and any others as were able to adapt to the changing conditions that killed off even those that were once the fittest. We may call the survivors lucky. Pathways to survival and development that kill off so many may strike us as a cruel. But cruel compared to what? When the environment changes, as it must, isn't it better for a few lucky (or chosen?) mutants to survive, and their progeny flourish, than for the whole species to go extinct? Many species go extinct anyway. Evolution is miraculous, but its harshness seems inconsistent with the benevolence that we attribute to God. I praise God for God's Creation, and do not criticize or judge or disbelieve in God if the process of Creation does not meet all my human standards. Surely God knows what God is doing and I don't.

* * *

To exist and advance, life has required harshness—earthquakes and floods and other natural disasters, plagues, carnivores, survival of the fittest and luckiest, extinction of the less fit or lucky, and so on. Likewise the "natural instincts" that helped our forebears to survive and evolve probably included the brutality, aggression, deceptiveness, and destructiveness that cause so much suffering today. God also created the ameliorating powers of love, peace, community, and maybe religion, to leaven the effects of the harsh instincts. Perverse people often pervert religion to justify their barbaric behavior.

* * *

According to Isaiah 11:6, "The wolf also shall dwell with the lamb, and the leopard shall lie down with the kid...." But if the wolf does not eat the lamb, it will starve. Same for the leopard and the baby goat. What do we think of the fact that many animals must kill and eat a great many other animals in order to survive? We rightly praise the Balance of Nature and fault the people who mess it up. Restoring wolves to Yellowstone National Park in 1995, for example, after they had been eliminated in the 1920s, reportedly benefited the otter, grizzly bear, rabbit, bee, song bird, and beaver populations, aspens, willows, the river banks, and much else in the park that had gone badly out of whack.

* * *

"God created man in his own image…." (Genesis 1:27) This claim, I suggest, cannot have been divinely inspired. The more we learn of the scope and marvels of Creation, the more absurd appears the claim that we puny humans are in the image of the Creator. Indeed, whoever makes or believes the claim needs to have an image of God in mind; but who has ever formed an adequate image of the Great Mystery to credibly make the claim?

* * *

Saying that we are created in God's image strikes me as a grandiose, presumptuous way of saying that there is a particle of God in each of us, which may be a presumptuous way of saying that there is in each of us an echo of God that can, if we let it, respond to or resonate with or do what is godly. Back in the ancient day, the wild animal part of our nature led to our survival and evolution; but in the end, it's the godly part that's needed if humanity is to survive.

* * *

Did life as we know it ignite from some confluence of particular molecules, warmth, and moisture? Was life infused from somewhere else in the universe, and, if so, how did it come into being out there and survive the journey to here? Or was dormant life awakened, or imprisoned life released, from within matter that we in our ignorance consider inanimate? Science keeps looking for how and where life on Earth began, but suppose it did not begin at any given time and place but existed ever since or even before what is commonly called the Big Bang? Perhaps life permeates all matter, just as atoms and subatomic particles do, but can come to fruition only under rare conditions of temperature, atmosphere, moisture, chemistry, and so on. Then the advent of these favorable conditions on Earth permitted the evolution of slugs and worms, then dolphins, cats, and dogs and other "intelligent" or higher animals, and, finally so far, the human body and brain. We may never know if latent life permeates everything, waiting to be released like the power of the atoms in the Bomb, but this may be at least as plausible as the accepted theory that at a certain point or points in time and place and confluence of necessary conditions, a spark of life ignited. Either theory may have been God's way of saying, "Let there be life." In any event, God created the cosmos and the exquisite conditions for sparks of life to flame and the flame to spark new life.

* * *

The theory that there is life in all matter seems to be consistent: with the Quaker view that there is That of God in every person; with the more common view that all life has value; with music being a universal language that anyone may respond to; and with the fact that flowers seem to flourish when people love them. Many of us look down on allegedly primitive tribes that believe that all kinds of things have their own spirits, but perhaps those tribes know more, and we less, than we suppose. Scholar of religions Huston Smith says that according to Islam, all matter is God; and I have heard Christians say the same. This universal life theory is consistent, too, with a prospect of life's going on after mortal death, a question being whether we continue as individuals or merge back into a common spirit or become whatever.

* * *

Only recently did scientists discover that there is amazing energy in matter (e=mc2). Will they discover there's also life in matter?

* * *

Consider the energy and profusion with which life bursts forth every Spring; the force of life and of the sex drive; the tenacity with which plants, animals, and most people cling to their lives. Perhaps life itself inheres in all matter—rocks and rivers—and *must* burst into being whenever and wherever in the cosmos circumstances permit.

* * *

Nothing is unnatural or supernatural. If it happens, it is natural. Even when it's sexual.

* * *

It strikes me as odd that some things are considered evil if people, in their ignorance, consider them "unnatural." They should only be considered evil if they're hurtful.

* * *

Anyone who wants further proof of how marvelously complex and well-engineered we humans are should watch an autopsy—preferably not on a person we knew—and note the glistening economy with which organs are packed into the torso and the other neat arrangements inside us.

* * *

They say that the devil is in the details, but when it comes to the wonders of the world, we may sense God in the details—among other places.

* * *

We like to think that the most favored form of life evolved (created) so far is we, the people. Perhaps we are right. Next come dolphins, whales, chimps, pigs, squirrels, and other "intelligent" or "higher" animals, and so on down the line. Humans are the only species I know of whose members may acknowledge, worship, honor, and thank God, and kill for pleasure.

* * *

It matters which creation story we believe, since the story suggests the magnitude of the gratitude that we owe to God for the Creation that includes us. We owe God more thanks and praise and appreciation for the Creation that science describes—that is, the real one—than for the ancient creation stories like Genesis or the accidental creation that atheists espouse.

* * *

The silently towering redwoods of California are cathedrals of God.

* * *

The ancient, basic question: Why is there something and not nothing? Many scientists say it's because of the Big Bang. That's all very interesting for *how* the cosmos happened, that is, for the process by which it came into being, but it does not answer the question of *why* God decided to create the cosmos.

* * *

I grew up during the Golden Age of radio dramas—*The Lone Ranger, The Shadow, I Love a Mystery*. But history teaches that a great many people did not love unsolved mysteries such as how and why we came to exist. So they adopted creation stories, myths, and doctrines to solve or eliminate these mysteries—all of which most of my Christian friends dismiss except for the versions contained in the Bible and Christian doctrine, which some of them believe and some don't. It's my observation that scientific discoveries have reduced the biblical creation account to a metaphor while omitting explanations of God's reasons for creating us. For myself, I have no doubt that God created all that is, but I can only guess at God's reasons.

* * *

Why did God create us? Religious philosopher Richard Shelburne speculates that "the beauty of the evolution of the inanimate world from the Big Bang (or from eternity) would be quite enough of a reason for [giving life to animals], even if God were the only person to have observed it. But he is not; we ourselves can now admire earlier and earlier stages of cosmic evolution through our telescopes."[9]

* * *

Sometimes we do things simply because we can. Did God craft the cosmos because God could, meeting the challenges of crafting it so intricately and well? What would God be doing with God's time and abilities if God did *not* create and perhaps intervene in the cosmos?

* * *

The fact that large masses of matter become spheres suggests that God intended from the get-go for the cosmos to include habitats on which life could flourishes. Imagine trying to survive the seasons on an Earth that was shaped as irregularly as an asteroid.

* * *

God evidently wanted to share with us humans and other creatures the gift of life that God presumably has. And with plants too, I suppose.

* * *

Perhaps rock music's Jefferson Airplane inadvertently got the reason God created us right when, in their 1960's classic *Somebody to Love,* they asked: "Don't you want somebody to love? Don't you need somebody to love? Wouldn't you love somebody to love? You better find somebody to love."

* * *

Many early churchmen thought that God created us in order to praise God, though I doubt that God is a narcissist or has an ego that needs praise. On the other hand, God deserves many thanks, and we would be remiss not to thank God.

* * *

There is a theory that God created us (and presumably intelligent beings on other planets) because God needs us to love God. A theory even claims that God courts people and if God fails to win our love, then God created the cosmos, including us, in vain.[10] While I cannot be certain that all this is false, it strikes me as approaching the height of naïve arrogance. In giving us free will, God must have known that some of us would love God and some wouldn't. If this weren't okay with God, I have to wonder whether God would have done it.

* * *

Did God create the vast symmetries and beauty that permeate the cosmos solely for God's self or for beings that we don't know about (angels?), or with us and other appreciative creatures in mind, or all of these reasons and maybe more?

* * *

Wondering why God created us may prompt the question, what is the purpose of our lives? Micah says that God wants us to do justly, love mercy, and walk humbly with our God. Jesus tells us to feed the hungry, clothe the naked, and visit the sick and imprisoned. Others tell us to work for peace, justice, and equality. But what if it someday comes to pass that peace and justice reign, equality prevails, poverty ends, and the other problems are solved? Not to worry. Since there's scant chance that humans will achieve such a Peaceable Kingdom, people who care about other people need never be bored.

* * *

Why have we received the gift of life? Perhaps God found it lonely or boring to exist without the company of some partly independent beings, however puny, for God to observe and even listen to. Perhaps it interests God, pleases God, amuses God, disappoints God, even stimulates God (if God can have such feelings) to see what we paltry humans think, say, and do. Same with other intelligent beings on other planets. Did God create us and endow us with a measure of free will, in part, to enable God to experience and sometimes enjoy points of view that agree with or differ from God's own, however limited, predictable, or foolish ours may be? Is it of any value to God to listen in on the thoughts of beings whose better thoughts may flash like fireflies across the night of time? Does human humor ever amuse God? Does God enjoy gossip even half as much as I do? No people, no gossip.

* * *

We owe everything to God. Does God owe anything to us?

* * *

Consider the fact that it's more blessed to give than to receive. May God have created the world and us, in part, in order to have beings to give to?

* * *

Does God enjoy the world the way some people enjoy a fancy set of electric trains? Or more because we are not confined to tracks? Or less because there's so much tragedy?

* * *

Most humans value sociability; does God? Loneliness is a human survival tool because it goads most of us to cleave together as groups, tribes, lovers, nations, and so on, in which we survive better than we do alone. But the fact that sociability helps people's survival does not mean that the presumably eternally surviving one God cannot be lonely, too, and prefers a sociability of sorts. Was it to keep God some kind of company that God created us discrete beings, however puny and inferior, and seems to insist on our having a measure of free will that often leads to trouble but without which we'd be wind-up toys, and so, even more predictable, boring, and less vibrant company than we are?

* * *

I delight in my progeny and their doings, and did so even back when they were very young and totally incompetent. So maybe God does too, at least when we aren't screwing up.

* * *

What would God have done with all God's intelligence and power and time if not create this cosmos and perhaps much else? What would God be doing if not keeping watch on the cosmos and its tenants and sometimes intervening? Probably plenty; but I hope that, overall, God takes pleasure in us, in spite of all the reasons we give God not to.

* * *

While it seems presumptuous and inaccurate to think that we humans were *the* object of Creation, I think it likely that we were *one of the objects* since we are among the improbable beings whose existence all the long-shot coincidences (i.e., God) made possible. In many ways we are the most accomplished beings that we know about. Also the most foolish. Which is all the more reason for supposing that God has created intelligent beings on other planets too and did not leave their creation entirely to random Chance or the chances that the Drake Equation posits.

* * *

It's fun to speculate on why God created the cosmos and us, but so long as God remains largely mysterious, God's reasons figure to remain mysterious too. And if some being ever explains them to us lucidly – perhaps an angel after we die—there's no guarantee that we are capable of comprehending them.

* * *

Consider the vastness of space; the pervasive cold; vast galaxies spinning through the void; the numberless balls of raging heat; the lumps of rock, iron, ice, and other matter zipping about; the solar systems of stars and planets that do not fly apart; the concentrations and diffusions of light, heat, and other energy; the miracles of water and carbon. What a hostile and unlikely place this is for anything as fragile and needy as life as we know it! What a warm, fruitful, benign planet we live upon! What a brilliant gift of God that we exist and even thrive!

* * *

If God wants to share life with all other creatures, is that reason enough for Creation?

* * *

Must Creation have a purpose? Must any of God's deeds have what we call a purpose? Must any of God's deeds have what we call a purpose? Since being purpose-driven seems to have served human survival, evolution, and prosperity, it's evident that we need purposes, but does God? I suspect yes but obviously can't be sure. Maybe the purpose of Creation is its dynamic existence, and nothing more. Whatever the purpose may have been, the results are magnificent.

* * *

Roaring, the 707 rose from the highway to nowhere like a javelin flung at the sky. Blue Pacific wheeled beneath the wing as we climbed back over the City of the Angels, Santa Catalina thrust purple through the ocean to the south. Still climbing, we crossed the crags and pines and glass houses of the San Bernardino Mountains. Straight roads through the sun-blasted Mojave Desert belied the look that no person could live down there, much less endeavor. All flights crossed the Grand Canyon when I would fly from JFK to LAX and return in the 1960s; and looking down I saw why. The snow-dappled Rockies rose beneath us and fell away as we reached green America. People must strive to be important in each tiny city that dots the endless land. If God conformed to current standards, God would have made those rivers straight. Lightning flashed pink and orange in a white wall ahead. The huge plane threaded between thunderheads like a minnow through a coral reef, through tomorrow's weather back East. Two centuries to cross America and four hours back. You who ask whether people were made to fly, ask rather whether God intended to withhold such beauty from us forever.

* * *

"The heavens declare the glory of God, and the firmament showeth his handiwork." Psalm 19. The psalmist knew only a tiny part of it, but got it right all the same.

Science

Hebrews wrote their Book of Genesis millennia ago. Scientists are still writing theirs—as a chapter in their Book of Revelation. Unlike Revelation in the Christian Bible, which abounds in symbols and some call a Book of Obscurity, theirs is a Book of Clarity, a work in progress that aims to describe the marvels that the Creator performed in giving us the benign planet that is home for all of us and vulgarians are currently despoiling.

* * *

Science does not repudiate God the Creator; rather, it sets forth far more wonders of God's Creation than the authors of the Scriptures ever imagined, dreamt, hallucinated, or said God told them.

* * *

Everyone who took science in high school knows more about the creation and nature of the cosmos and life on Earth than did any of the founders of the world's great religions or the authors of the Judeo-Christian Scriptures or anyone born more than a few centuries ago.

* * *

Thanks to modern physics, astronomy, biology, and other sciences,, today's high school students can learn more than Jesus and the Scripture writers ever knew about the wonders of Creation. We need to teach the basics of astronomy and biology in Sunday schools, as well as high schools, so that our children can properly learn and appreciate these wonders and their Creator. Too largely, though, Sunday schools teach the ancient myths and ignore the wonderous facts.

* * *

The more that all of us learn about these subjects, the better able we are to appreciate the mighty achievements of the Being who asks us to do justly, love mercy, and walk humbly with our God. (Micah 6:8)

* * *

Science describes and often explains how the Creator did it and does it. Yet we would be foolish if science leads us to dismiss the wisdom, warmth, humanity, and profundity of the Bible.

* * *

Take care about embracing too fervently the vast array of scientific discoveries lest we lose sight of the wisdom of the ages and the human truths contained in the Scriptures.

* * *

In his book *Why Religion Matters*, Huston Smith defines *science* as "the body of facts about the natural world that controlled experiments *require us to believe*, together with logical extrapolations from those facts, and the added things that scientific instruments enable us to see with our own eyes."[11] This definition, though not complete, works for what follows.

Note Smith's words *require us to believe*, even though more accurate science often displaces previous science, meaning we are often "required" to believe stuff that turns out to be untrue. I don't feel required to believe in the Big Bang, as I understand that theory, though I know it may turn out to be as correct as some eminent scientists now claim.

* * *

It's worth remaining mindful that science is fallible; its theories often evolve or are disproved or superseded. Many people who are in the thrall of science give it undue credit, thinking that it explains what it merely describes or that it will eventually explain everything. Physicians describe the effects of aspirin; they have yet to explain them.

* * *

The more one learns about the marvels through which today's world came into being—not from Genesis, but from astronomy, physics, geology, biology, Darwinian evolution, and so on—the harder it must be to conclude that a host of interdependent long-shot chances created all things great and small in the cosmos. Conversely, ignorance of such marvels facilitates atheism.

* * *

A popular myth (naïve assumption) has it that science will sooner or later solve all our problems. But many problems are insoluble. And science has yet to solve the common cold.

* * *

Science does not conflict with religion except for those who insist on taking Scriptures literally, no matter the evidence to the contrary. St. Augustine of Hippo held that when the Book of Scripture conflicts with the Book of Nature, Scripture must be reinterpreted. How sensible!

* * *

To elaborate: According to Karen Armstrong among others, St. Augustine held that whenever the literal meaning of Scripture clashes with reliable scientific information, the integrity of science must be respected; a Scripture should be reinterpreted if it appears to clash with proven science. Armstrong went on to say that this Augustinian principle "would dominate biblical interpretation in the West until well into the early modern period."[12] It astonishes me that great numbers of today's Christians reject St. Augustine's sensible approach and cling to a literal reading of Scriptures in the face of all the evidence that God's creation is far more marvelous than the Scriptures relate or Augustine understood. Thus literalists sell God short.

* * *

Saint Augustine and others tell us that passages of Scripture that cannot be taken literally should be reinterpreted, taken symbolically, and so on. But some passages are simply wrong, and no amount of reinterpretation can save them.

* * *

The revelations of science bolster one's faith in a Creator at least to the extent that they demonstrate the Creator's genius and the virtual impossibility that Creation happened without this Being. Before science had illuminated so much about the world, people could not have seen the world as being nearly as miraculous as we see it today. And scientific revelations roll on.

* * *

Happily, science has provided us with these newly discovered reasons for believing in God, the Creator, at a time when humankind seems much in need of such well-grounded belief.

* * *

Genesis has us humans starting out fully evolved and unsullied in an earthly paradise called Eden. But the sciences show that the opposite was true, leaving room for hope that a real Eden may yet lie ahead if enough people keep on trying to make the world a better place.

* * *

The Old and New Testaments purport to suggest God's power by describing various deeds that defy the laws of Nature that God created—the sun stood still for Joshua, Jesus walked on water and revived cadavers, etc. But then as now, people may see God's power in the hills and oceans and deserts, the heavens, and the faces of us people, all reflecting the plenitude of Nature. The more of reality and natural history that we see, the more we may glimpse of God.

* * *

Throughout history, people have been glimpsing the face of God in Nature, most likely because it's there.

* * *

Actions reveal character, though less for the incomprehensible Being than for most human beings. By God's fruits may we know God, and perhaps by the whispers of the still small voice, insofar as it is given to people to know God at all.

* * *

Intelligent design: The more that science discovers, the smarter the Creator looks.

* * *

Isaac Newton said that we see through Nature to God. Rousseau, too, saw God in Nature's designs. So did Galileo. Einstein studied science, he said, to learn the mind of God.[13] Likewise, theoretical physicist and biologist Paul Davies writes: "Through science and mathematics, we can, so to speak, glimpse the mind of God.... And if you imagine playing the role of God and you have some sort of machine in front of you..., twiddle one knob, make the electron a bit heavier; twiddle another knob and make the strong nuclear force a bit stronger—you soon discover that you have to fine-tune those settings to extraordinary precision for there to be life." The indomitable Stephen Hawking said, "If we do discover a theory of everything..., we would truly know the mind of God."[14] No, we wouldn't, but we would have taken a step in that direction.[iv]

* * *

Einstein: "Science without religion is lame. Religion without science is blind."[15]

* * *

Science and religion complement each other. Science, at its best, describes what God has done. Religion, at its best, tells us what we had best do. Neither reveals why God created us.

* * *

---

iv I suppose that referring to "the mind of God" is as inadequate as describing God by lofty human adjectives; and what some call God's mind is very different from, and more marvelous than, what we humans think of as a mind.

Everyone else's creation story is a myth. Ours is the inerrant word of God. Lucky us!

* * *

All peoples have seemed to need a creation story; and the ancient Hebrews, like many other societies, created theirs ages before science began to describe reality accurately. Unlike Richard Dawkins, Sir Fred Hoyle, Sir Martin Rees (all of whom I cite in the essay on Atheism), and many more of today's scientists, the people who wrote the Book of Genesis were correct about the fundamental fact that God created the world and all living creatures. These ancient authors were, I believe, sound on other levels too. But they, like the authors of other venerable creation stories, simply didn't know enough to get all facts right. They apparently doped out Creation as best they could; but since they claimed that God authored their creation story, it has been very hard for great numbers of the faithful to stop believing it, even in the face of irrefutable proof that it didn't happen the way Genesis says it did. On the other hand, the falsity of these creation stories makes non-believers out of many people who don't see beyond them.

* * *

We live in a Golden Age of God's revelation through science, though it does not seem to be commonly recognized as such. Rather, many Christians resist the revelations of science that do not accord with scriptural accounts, and many who accept the science won't accept an incorporeal Creator whose existence cannot be proved to an absolute certainty. For the former, it's the old story, I know what I believe, so don't confuse me with the facts. For the latter, it's, I accept only absolute certainty. Well, that's your loss, not mine.

* * *

Science praises the Creator by revealing wonders of Creation that are far more astonishing, intricate, and miraculous than those contained in the accounts ("creation myths") that various religions devised. Rather than rejecting or ignoring the discoveries of science, religions need to embrace them as the revelations of Divine handiwork that they are.

* * *

Schools should light a flame in students, a thirst for knowledge, that will burn unquenched as long as they live. I feel blest that mine did so for me. The better we understand God's Creation, the better.

* * *

Only by embracing what science shows us can clerics compose proper prayers of gratitude and praise to God.

* * *

Much of literature is a serendipitous marriage of God's and people's creativity.

* * *

For some, it seems, God is mystery in a narrow sense: no mystery, no God. Once science solves some mystery of the universe or the atom or whatever, the people who equate God with factual mystery conclude that each new scientific discovery *pro tanto* diminishes God—whereas it is actually human ignorance about God's handiwork that is diminished.

* * *

Science has yet to explain much and will never explain all.

* * *

Though science describes much of how God did it and does it, science has its limits. It will never explain all phenomena nor solve all problems. Though scientific discovery has been experiencing a Golden Age, the age is bound to taper off, though not as fast as many predict.

* * *

Science has had such a good run during recent centuries that today many people entertain a naïve trust, bordering perhaps on idolatry, that science can and will solve all problems—safe energy; climate change; limited resources; the care and feeding of the ballooning human horde; drug-resistant diseases; answers to all questions about the cosmos, the atom, and so on. But science cannot and will not do all this. Faith that science will solve all problems is as naïve and bound to disappoint as is faith that God will protect good people from all bad things.

* * *

Whatever is, is natural.

* * *

Some people presume to measure God by science, but science cannot to be a test of God, lest we raise science into a god above God. Science, though, often tests what people say about God; and their words often fail the test. Does it serve God to cling to error about God's Creation?

* * *

Humility: A Master of Balliol College is said to have said, "What I don't know isn't knowledge." Similarly, some scientists deny the existence of what they have yet to discover, measure, quantify, or bottle. If they deny God because they have not proved God, why not, for the same reason, deny love?

* * *

Science on occasion colludes with ignorance in holding that stuff that science has yet to prove does not exist. Like extrasensory perception. Yet science learns stuff every day that has existed all along, silently waiting to be discovered or proved. While science may not have proved the existence of God to scientific certainty, it would be folly to conclude that therefore God does not exist. Will some scientist ever prove God's existence to that degree? I hope not.

* * *

From my Quakerly perspective, it seems that God and the bit of God within everyone permitted the founders and scribes of several great religions to know that God exists and created everything and loves us and makes life best when we love each other. God and the bit of God permitted those people to come to understand the most godly ways to live one's life and treat other people. The serene and priceless treasure of this wisdom remains as sound and timeless as ever. Both the mythic explanations of antiquity and the most astonishing discoveries of science testify to the glory of God's handiwork.

* * *

It is ironic that the same science that constantly reveals new marvels of Creation also convinces many people that a Creator does not exist. As science serves the faithful who remain open to new revelation, it also serves atheists.

* * *

An unmanned space probe called Galileo discovered evidence that beneath the shell of ice that covers the moon of Jupiter called Europa, there are tides of water that rise and fall nearly a hundred feet each cycle, thus creating fault lines about six hundred miles long in the ice.[16]

I assume there are many, many planets, and moons like Jupiter's, where physical conditions are so harsh that if any life exists, it is only in the most primitive forms. So far as we now know, human life as it has evolved on Earth is a pinnacle of God's physical creation. All the more reason for humans to stop mucking up the Earth and risking extinction by nukes.

* * *

Perhaps evolution works like breeding racehorses: natural selection aided by a skilled breeder. Consider how well the balances of Nature often work where people have not intervened.

* * *

Natural selection and mutations and the luck attending them are only the tip of the iceberg of all that it took to create and evolve human life. If the cosmos and the Sun and carbon and water and genes and DNA and warm Earth did not work as they do, no evolution, no us.

* * *

Some people attribute every aspect of every human and other animal into the natural selection and survival of the fittest theory, perhaps because Darwinism has become an idol in the temple of science.

* * *

The Large Hadron Collider is a 17-mile-long circular tunnel, mostly under Switzerland and partly under France. Mighty magnets inside it accelerate tiny particles called protons to a speed that is more than 99% the speed of light. These particles, zipping in opposite directions and completing the 17-mile circuit nearly 11,000 times per second, inevitably smash into each other producing tiny fireballs, which detectors inside the collider analyze. The European Organization for Nuclear Research (CERN) employed two teams of 3,000 physicists each to work with the collider in seeking to discover the infinitesimal and elusive Higgs boson, (a) the existence of which had been proposed by Peter Higgs of the University of Edinburgh and five other physicists in 1964, and (b) which would confirm the existence of a field of force (the Higgs field) that permeates space and gives mass to other subatomic particles such as the electron. Without mass, electrons would not bind to atoms and there would be no stars, planets, or us. At last on July 4, 2012, CERN announced that its scientists had, to a high degree of certainty, established the existence of the Higgs boson or at least a Higgs-boson-like particle.[v] This astonishing accomplishment by all those CERN scientists, I reflected, was as though 6,000 carpenters, using materials, forces, tools, and their own intelligence, all of which the Architect had made available to them, uncovered yet another vital component that the Architect had brilliantly devised in creating the cosmos and us.

* * *

"The Higgs boson discovery says nothing about religion," said Professor Lisa Randall, an accomplished theoretical physicist teaching at Harvard. The discovery was, she said, "a tribute to science and the ingenuity

---

v Dennis Overbye described the discovery dramatically and at length in an 8-page section of the March 5, 2013, *New York Times*. Hadrons are subatomic particles. Officially, the word Large in the collider's name describes bulky hadrons, though it also obviously describes the collider itself, which was the world's largest so far. According to the *Times* article, bosons are particles that can transmit forces between other particles.

of both theorists and experimenters that such a prediction could be made and verified. The discovery is truly inspirational—in a scientific way."[17] But which is more inspirational, the teams that made the discovery or the Creator that made the boson?

* * *

Whatever its errors on the details, Genesis got the main fact right: God created everything. Many scientists get the details right but miss the main fact.

* * *

Why is there something and not nothing? Because of God's inscrutable will and vast power. This doesn't answer the question, but it's the best I can do.

Atheism

Members of a popular faith burgeon across the land. Like many people of other persuasions, they believe that theirs is the one true faith. It surprises me how numerous they are, considering the leap of faith they must take in order to believe what they do in the face of reason, probabilities, and the world they see around them. For they are atheists. For them Chance alone generated the elements and created the cosmos and the myriad finely tuned intricacies that brought the cosmos and us to our present incredible condition.

* * *

Comedian George Carlin, posing as a football announcer, gave what he called a partial score, "Notre Dame 27." In like manner, many people ask a partial question, Is there a God? The complete question is, Is there a God, or did all Creation happen by chance? It strikes me that these are the only plausible options. If by chance, where did chance get the venue in which and materials with which to create?

* * *

Atheists claim that chance has done improbably amazing things with the materials at hand, but no reasonable atheist claims that chance created these materials. So why is there something and not nothing, and how did the something we call the cosmos come to exist?

* * *

Did God create this wide, wonderful world from the Big Bang (or whatever it was) onwards? Many people ponder the reasons for answering yes or no. Fewer turn to the question's essential complement: Or did Chance – meaning, chance after chance after chance – create everything? Was it Chance or God that created the sweep and complexity and all the wonders of matter and energy and life and love? Thinking thus on such questions, one may perhaps see how vast a leap of faith it takes to attribute Creation to a perfect concatenation of chances.

* * *

At some point before there was everything, it seems likely there was nothing. If so, could Chance have created everything out of nothing? Or did this feat require an intelligence and power that many call God?

* * *

It's either faith in God or faith in Chance, and the latter strikes me as being blind to logic and the realities of Creation.

* * *

Dennis Overbye, the cosmic affairs correspondent for the New York Times, told his readers on January 8, 2024:

"Galaxies are the city-states of the cosmos. Within the visible universe are an estimated two trillion of them, each containing as many as a trillion stars. But the visible universe is only a fraction of what's out there. Most of the matter in the cosmos seems to be in the form of dark matter; whatever dark matter is, it constitutes the invisible bones of the universe we see."

So, dear Atheists, chance may direct the fate of some stuff that already exists, but how, pray tell, did chance manage to bring all that matter and vast space in between it into being?

* * *

Many atheists apparently believe that life just sort of happened, that the essential combination of physical elements, warmth, and absorbable or digestible nutrients, each in the necessary gaseous or liquid or solid state, each possessing the other necessary attributes, somehow came into being all by themselves, managed to find each other, and, pouf, a spark of life spontaneously ignited in inanimate matter; and we are, in the words of a Cole Porter song, "a chemical reaction, that's all." A chemical reaction, moreover, that has managed to keep reproducing itself in a zillion species.

* * *

The mathematical symmetry that underlies so much of Nature. Pythagoras's right triangle. Kepler's sweep of the planets. The solid, liquid, gas, and plasma states of matter. The ability of atoms to use each other's electrons to form substances wholly different from their components. Einstein's e=mc2 and all the other neat laws of physics. The beauty and mathematics of music. All here by chance?

* * *

If there were no Creator, would we not expect chaos or nothingness rather than the laws of physics to prevail throughout the known universe? Of course, if chaos or nothingness prevailed, we would not be here to expect anything.

* * *

If cleanliness is next to godliness for believers, does cleanliness come first for atheists?

* * *

Did Creation self-generate? If it all happened by chance, Chance needed *something* to work with—specifically, primordial hydrogen and helium. How did these gases come into being? If you answer, the Big Bang, how did it come into being? And who or what endowed the simple elements with the potential to transmute over billions of years and zillions of exploding stars eventually into us? For the physical world to be created in conformity with the laws of physics and mathematics and so on, where did those laws come from? Needn't *something else* have created or imposed them? Same questions for the essential forces such as gravity, electromagnetism, and the waves that comprise heat, light, and sound. How could Chance have created matter or energy or forces or laws of Nature?

* * *

I understand that some atheists focus on one component of Creation, namely, evolution; and they conclude that since its processes of natural selection, mutation, and so on *could* have produced us humans by chance, then they *must* have produced us by chance; therefore there is no God. But besides being a logical non sequitur, such a focus on evolution is far too narrow. Where did the raw materials of evolution and the place(s) in which it could happen originate? Realistically, one must look to the whole of Creation: to everything from the so-called Big Bang onwards; for it was upon all of these conditions that our evolution, however chancy, has depended. As I tried to suggest in the fable of the Carpenter, the more aspects of the whole story that one considers, the less plausibly can one attribute it all to Chance. Unless, I suppose, a person has faith in atheism that's as impervious as a devotion to a cult leader.

* * *

Atheist Richard Dawkins, who is an evolutionary biologist, agrees that "chance is not the likely designer [because] the greater the statistical implausibility, the less plausible is chance as a solution." He argues, however, that the options for a theory of life are not "designer and chance. They are designer, chance and natural selection."[18]

But the elements of life had to exist before they could be naturally selected. You can't select apples from an empty bin. What created all those above-mentioned preconditions and ingredients that natural selection needed for doing its job? And what provided natural selection with a venue to work in, and what *only then* caused the spark of life to ignite in the simplest one-cell creature(s) so that natural selection could begin?[vi]

* * *

Paradoxically, as science discovers more and more of the marvels of Creation, many people invoke this same science to support their belief that it was Chance, not a vastly intelligent Being, that created it all. I suspect that some people do this because science shows them that creation as described in Genesis did not happen. But God's existence does not depend on the accuracy of an ancient explanation that was conceived in factual ignorance and bound to err.

* * *

Many atheists are well educated even though, paradoxically, ignorance nourishes atheism to the extent that the more one learns about the wonders of Creation, the harder it must be to disbelieve in a Creator.

* * *

Many atheists call people who believe in God naïve. I think it's atheists who are naïve if they believe that this wondrous world came into being through one improbable chance after another after another. In the same vein, some people seem to feel it's déclassé or unsophisticated or a mark of ignorance to admit they believe in God. While such a stance may make them feel superior to those they consider faithful, it is one of the least reasonable reasons for denying God.

* * *

Devotees of science who will not acknowledge that a powerful intelligence underlay Creation are, again paradoxically, like the anti-science know-nothings who will not accept global climate change until it's proved to a mathematical certainty—if then.

* * *

I would not be surprised if atheism flourishes best in cities, where people are largely removed from Nature and surrounded by manmade symmetries. But my old friend Sylvia Farmer Hultkrans responds, "Maybe so, but I found living in NYC made me more compassionate and sensitive because of the diversity, crowds of humanity on the streets and subways." Amen.

---

vi If scientists someday ignite such a spark in their laboratory, that fine achievement will still beg the question of what endowed the ingredients with the capacity to be coaxed into life.

* * *

Some atheism may reflect the wishful thinking of people who won't or can't face the apparent contradictions of God, or of what they have been led to believe about God.

* * *

Great expectations: Praising God by describing God with the adjectives *omniscient* plus *omnipotent* plus *benevolent*, while surely well-meant and probably partly sound, disserves both God and people to the extent that sooner or later many of us notice that this God of Our Adjectives does not exist. Highly praising God thus leads some folks to stop believing in God.

* * *

So does tragedy. It seems that many people stop believing in God when they discover that the assurances they have received that God will protect them, and maybe their loved ones, turn out to be untrue. But this is a man-made god, it does not exist, and these disillusioned people are probably sound to stop believing in it. Unfortunately, many of them then stop believing in any god at all including the real One. For them, it's good God or no God, as they define *good*.

* * *

Many people seem serenely able to maintain their faith in God no matter how terrible the tragedies that befall others—the loss of someone else's child, the Holocaust, wars in which their children do not serve and die, epidemics and earthquakes in other lands, and so on. But let such a tragedy befall *them* or a person they love and, lo, their faith vanishes.[vii] They stop believing in the god that has been misrepresented to them. It's better, I suggest, to reshape your concept of God if you can, or to be disappointed in or angry with God—which I suppose God understands and probably expects—than to deprive yourself of faith in God and deprive God of your thanks for God's gifts, which, in spite of life's tragedies, are marvelous.

* * *

Though atheism and skepticism sometimes arise when the real God differs from the god that we imagine or were taught to believe in, what kind of a god would mold itself to fit the imaginings of humans?

* * *

---

vii Even though the terrorist attack of 9/11/2001 directly affected relatively few people, many other Americans reportedly took it so personally that they lost their faith in God. Who, they fancied, always protects the USA.

The fact that good people often suffer serves as argument that God does not exist, when what it actually shows is that God is not as many of us have been led to believe.

* * *

Many people who deny, rebel against, attack, or are disillusioned by man-created images of God and the myths and errors in the Bible, never give the real God a chance. Instead of rejecting the flawed orthodoxies they were taught during their trustful childhoods, they forego the possibility of enriching their lives with faith. Which I suspect is less God's loss than theirs.

* * *

There seems to be a vicious circle, or a descending spiral: As hosts of reasonable people have turned secular, the care and feeding of religion has been left increasingly to people who are not burdened by either doubt about their perceived truths or restraint in imposing their truths on others. While they may sincerely believe they are being godly, they eschew uncertainty and humility at whatever cost to their neighbors. Perhaps we need a new commandment: Butt out.

* * *

Some critics of the theory that the wonders of Nature reveal some of God's handiwork point to Nature's perceived imperfections, claiming, for instance, that we humans are so imperfect that "God" could not have created us. But we are already incredibly marvelous beings, and each person is a temple of God, even though we apparently remain works in progress, still evolving; and there is no sound reason to suppose that meeting some narrow, biased, human notion of perfection accords with God's wishes. Either God meets our standards of perfection, or God does not exist. Really?

* * *

Many atheists seem fond of arguing that much of the Bible is factually wrong about Nature and history, and that much evil has been done in the name of religion. However much truth there is in these arguments—a lot, I think—they have no logical bearing on the questions of whether God exists or intervenes, and how we should treat our fellows.

* * *

Does the unbroken gray of an overcast sky convince us that the Sun is not shining in the blue beyond? Does a perceived dearth of convincing proof convince us there is no God?

* * *

Some atheists say that ancient peoples created religious myths out of their deep need to believe in a god. This sounds likely but has no bearing on whether or not God exists.

* * *

Before signing off on this book, I thought I'd better read a well-regarded case for atheism. Turning to *God Is Not Great* by Christopher Hitchens,[19] I found myself in agreement with much of what he says, particularly his critiques of many orthodox beliefs and of the vast savagery committed over the centuries in the names of God and Jesus. But these critiques of what humans have believed and done fail to show that God does not exist.[viii]

* * *

A better book is *The God Delusion* by Richard Dawkins. He argues similar points, says that the God described in the Old Testament doesn't sound like a nice guy, and raises the question, If there is a Designer, who designed the Designer? Dawkins's question argues, in effect, that either the Designer had a designer or the Designer does not exist.[20] Poppycock! And his question ignores the possibility—I would say likelihood—that God always existed, so had no need to be designed. Most significantly, he fails to face the questions, If there was no Creator, where did everything come from and who arranged for the ways it works?

* * *

I suspect that atheists like Hitchens and Dawkins love the god of early Scriptures because that god presents a fat target, relatively easy to shoot holes in and pick apart.

* * *

A Presbyterian minister named Beverly Brewster wrote in a letter to the editor in the January 8, 2013, *New York Times*, "I often say to self-proclaimed atheists, 'Tell me more about the God you don't believe in. I'm pretty sure I don't believe in that God either.'" It sounds as though Reverend Brewster doesn't believe in the god of Hitchens and Dawkins. I know I don't.

* * *

Carbon is an essential element of life as we know it. Referring to the eminent scientist Sir Fred Hoyle, science writer Timothy Ferris wrote: "Were the carbon resonance level only 4 percent lower, carbon atoms wouldn't form in the first place. Were the oxygen resonance only half a percent higher, virtually

---

viii Hitchens' subtitle is How Religion Poisons Everything. Finding this canard an absurd exaggeration, I would amend it to read How Abuses of Religion Poison Much.

all the carbon ... would have combined with helium to form oxygen. No carbon, no us.... Hoyle says that his atheism ... was shaken by this discovery."[21] So Hoyle's atheism was shaken by these two long shots (which I don't claim to understand beyond their being just right), but it took not only these two but also many, many more long shots harmonizing in the serendipitous concert that created life as we know it.

* * *

The British cosmologist and astrophysicist Sir Martin Rees wrote a book, called *Just Six Numbers: The Deep Forces that Shape the Universe* (2000), that views the past and likely future of the universe through a lens of six factors—such as the strength of the electrical force that holds atoms together, and the relationship between the energy expanding the universe and the gravity pulling it back—which, had they been any larger or smaller, or stronger or weaker, would have rendered stars and planets and life impossible. "Is this tuning," he asks, "just a brute fact, a coincidence? Or is it the providence of a benign Creator? I take the view that it is neither. An infinity of universes may well exist where the numbers are different." So, his theory goes, out of this infinity of universes, one of them, ours, chanced to get all the key numbers right—much like the monkeys that finally typed out *Moby Dick*. Rees is not alone in placing his faith in such a multiverse, even though he concedes that it is "still conjectural, still no more than a tentative hypothesis."[22] This strikes me as a mighty stretch to avoid a clear conclusion. And if by any chance such a multiverse exists, what created it?

* * *

If scientists discover a so-called multiverse comprised of many universes that cannot sustain life, in addition to ours that can and does, the question becomes, Who created all of them? If God created something that people cannot see the point of, then God does not exist? Fiddledeedee! The existence of universes that some humans presume to consider useless would have no bearing on whether God exists or created those universes, for God knows what reason.

* * *

Take the basic question, why is there something and not nothing? Believers may say, Because God chose to create it. Atheists, I suggest, offer no such plausible explanation.

* * *

Einstein believed in God the Creator through the workings of Creation, but he did not believe in God the Intervener because he did not believe that God would break rules of physics that God had established.[23] (There are, of course, many ways to intervene without breaking these rules, such as people's narrow escapes from harm, their unexplained impulses to do things that turns out well, the happy coincidences we encounter, and so on.) Many people, similarly disbelieving in God the Intervener, therefore reject the existence of God the Creator—which does not follow. A Christian must by definition believe that God has intervened at least to the extent of sending or inspiring Jesus.

* * *

An old friend who is an atheist told me, after reading this chapter, that he agrees with nearly everything I say in it. Yet he remains an atheist.

* * *

It would not surprise me if God intended to leave enough room for doubt about God's own existence so that a respectable number of people will reasonably conclude that God does not exist, and the rest of us remain free to choose which, if any, faith to follow. If so, these atheists are part of God's plan.

* * *

All people are precious, whether or not they believe in God. We know that many non-believers are more kind, compassionate, and helpful than many believers.

* * *

May we respect each other's sincerely held beliefs about God and nearly everything else, whether or not we agree.

Religion

For the most part, the basic truths about religion, like those about life, have long since been expressed. Yet revelation continues. Spiritual truths flow from the discoveries of scientists and psychologists, from considering more faiths than one's own, and from shaking free of questionable doctrines of the past. A spreading assumption that God values every person equally, plus the marvels of cell phones and the Internet, make the profundities that may issue from the most humble person on Earth more likely than ever to be widely heeded, which is still not likely.

* * *

Ancient Scriptures enrich people with their wisdom and beauty, yet basing one's religion on them constricts one with the ignorance and biases (e.g., machismo) of their ancient authors. Much ancient wisdom is eternal; some of it fails to fit new situations; some of it is unwise. Arnold Toynbee pointed out long ago that societies, like animals, either adapt and evolve to meet ever changing circumstances or they die. Sometimes, it seems, the folks who run a religion either stunt or stop its essential evolution—based, I suppose, on the theory that divinely revealed truth can't change. Take the widespread teachings against effective birth control, which means encouraging both abortions and the population explosion that threatens human survival.

* * *

Religions tend to look backwards to their founding myths, for who can doubt what tradition says God said? But ancient peoples formed their religions from sparse and faulty knowledge of how Earth and everything on it came into being; and theologians who regard the ancient texts as being divinely inspired have often failed to adapt their certainties to the recent revelations of physicists, astronomers, geologists, archaeologists, chemists, and Darwinian evolutionists who show us the marvels of what God actually did and does. But when it comes to the mysteries of the human heart, the ancients, like many peoples we call primitive, may have known as much as we do or much more.

* * *

A hazard of *not* looking back is that we forsake the wisdom of the ages and relegate ourselves to reinventing the wheel of life.

* * *

If freedom of religion means anything, it means freedom to err.

* * *

The godliness of certain religious sages led them to reach many sound and even inspired conclusions about how to live our lives and treat our fellows—as sound today as they were when written. Love our neighbors. Forgive those who trespass against us. God, however, did not dictate the particulars of physics, astronomy, chemistry, or biology to those sages. On these subjects, they presumably did the best they could and maybe more than they had to. Then they or their supporters claimed that the resulting accounts-stories-myths came from God. But if they came from God, one supposes that they would have been accurate.

* * *

Some of the great religions reflect human gropings towards an understanding of God, the unknowable. (I understand that God or gods are not central to Buddhism, Confucianism, Taoism, and non-theist Quakers.) But any approach to understanding requires that one first know the world that God created. The founding prophets of the major religions knew their fellow humans quite well, and this knowledge informs the sacred texts that contain their wisdom (and in the Bible, at least, considerable sexism); but they knew little of the physical world beyond what they could see, hear, smell, and touch; and their ignorance laced those texts with errors.

* * *

For me, the soundness of a religion ought to be measured, not by its creation story nor by any claimed relationship between God and its chief prophet, but by the ways in which it encourages us to do for each other, refrain from doing to each other, and accept the reality that every one of us is a creature of God.

* * *

Brother Michael of the Weston Priory in Vermont observed that a religion's authenticity should be judged, not on the number of its adherents, but on whether it espouses certain beliefs such as non-violence.

* * *

"Service to mankind is the highest form of religion."

—Frederick Law Olmstead,
who designed New York City's Central Park.

* * *

Many accept the perceived Word of God; fewer accept the risks that it invites. Many admire the Good Samaritan, but who today stops to help the ragged, stinking, potentially violent or deranged person lying in a dark doorway?

* * *

I doubt that God wants us killing or even berating each other over points of doctrine that God knows we can't be sure about. If we see others err, so what? Who is free from error?

* * *

How many battles would have been avoided and lives spared if religious leaders through the ages had admitted, "Actually, God did not tell me" this or that point of doctrine!

* * *

When an ideology becomes a secular religion, as capitalism has for many Americans—I'm thinking particularly but not exclusively of the wealthiest One Percent—it becomes idolatry. To a degree, capitalism and Marxism are rival altars in the temple of Mammon.

* * *

Serious religions would do well to recognize the science that accurately describes God's handiwork and embrace this science as being the bearer of divine revelation that it is.

* * *

The psalmists and other authors of the Bibles who were soundly moved to praise God knew relatively little and misperceived much about the wonders of God's works. Now that science has uncovered many of these wonders, many people who are convinced or contented to be irreligious pay the wonders little heed. Many even use these revelations to deny that the God who caused them exists. Like, who needs God when science has the answers? Yeah, right.

* * *

Sincerely believing one or another creation myth as the true account of events closes off many faithful people from marveling at the vastly greater wonders of God's actual creation. On the other hand, people who use scientific discoveries to reject these myths may dump the baby with the bath water and reject the wisdom residing in the myths.

* * *

A similar curiosity has apparently motivated both the ancient mythmakers and today's scientists.

* * *

Christianity, Judaism, and Islam venerate segments of the Middle Eastern real estate for events that happened upon them long ago. Yet people's doings seldom change the earth beneath their feet except when they create a hole in it or spill blood on it. It is hard to imagine that God or Jesus or Mohammed would want anyone to hate or fight or kill over so-called sacred places, however historically significant, especially places that the ages have altered beyond recognition or rendered impossible to locate with any certainty. In Jerusalem in 1993, a tour guide told Nancy and me that the Last Supper or the Crucifixion or some other biblical event occurred over here unless it was over there. What matters is how we treat each other, and people have often treated each other badly over these patches of land. We never truly possess any land, although a tiny parcel will someday possess many of us.

* * *

Perhaps most people espouse one religion or another, or believe theirs is the best or only one, not from a reasoned or impassioned choice, but from accidents of birth and ignorance of the alternatives. But today vast numbers of people have the chance to fairly consider religions other than their own. With improved communications, especially radio, TV, paperback books, and the Internet—for instance, Huston Smith's book, *The World's Great Religions*—the opportunities for real choice have increased, at least for people who are open to learning about and considering them. May this lead to "cherry-picking" of what we consider the best of several religions? Of course. We thus increase our chances of seeing commonalities among religions and, dare we admit it, finding elements of other religions that we perceive as being more godly than our own.

* * *

Each major religion bears studying for what it tells us about ourselves, each other, how to live, and perhaps about God. But no religion has a monopoly on the truth—as should be obvious from the truths that the main religions share. Accepting any one religion whole seems certain to make a believer at least partly wrong, as we may readily see by looking at any religion except our own—whichever our own happens to be. On the other hand, rejecting any major religion whole also invites error. Picking and choosing among their elements may be hazardous—and may be called "cherry-picking" as if that were bad—but it also invites us to find a fuller Truth.

* * *

We have our natural selves and our better selves. It is a major job of parents, society, and religion to tame the former and nurture the latter in their children. Their failure to do so may stunt their children for the rest of their lives and perhaps hereafter.

* * *

Religion, when abused, may become a two-edged sword: it should help us tame our destructive instincts, not inflame them as it often does. Consider Europeans' Crusades, the Inquisition, and the spiritual aggression attending European's barbaric colonization, decimation, and exploitation of the peoples of Africa, the Western Hemisphere, and much of Asia.

* * *

It's clear that religion *should* appeal to people's better natures. But rather than helping us to rise above our lower selves, religions as preached and practiced often divert us with rituals, dogmas, bromides, abstractions, and theological niceties that, implicitly or explicitly, bless an inequitable status quo or an outright aggression. Reverend Feelgood may fill the pews, but he misses the point.

* * *

Beyond question, religions have caused much harm. In an article in the *Harvard Divinity Bulletin* that focused on "the sheer horror of the Catholic clergy sexual abuse crisis," Professor of Religious Studies and History Robert A. Orsi asks: "Would we who are scholars of religion not all agree ... that on balance, in the long perspective of human history, religions have done more harm than good and that the good that they do is almost always inseparable from the harm? I think we would."[24]

With all respect, I, who am not a scholar of religion, would not agree.

My differences with Dr. Orsi et al. lie first in the fact that I differentiate the harm that religion itself has done from the harm that predatory or misguided men and women have done *in the name of religion*—the Crusades, the Inquisition and other slaughters of alleged heretics, countless wars over religious differences, human sacrifices to propitiate imagined gods, Catholic priests raping children and bishops covering up and thus enabling more crimes, nuns whacking pupils with rulers. Yet taking due account of the harm that is not fairly attributable to religion but to "a *distortion* of [religion's] true identity or of its essence" fails to dissuade Dr. Orsi.

Second, religions have done vast good, which *there is no way* he can have quantified, through the peace, love, solace, and guidance that millions and perhaps billions of people have found in their faiths; he allows that he himself "was raised in a devout Italian Catholic home." Third, most peoples throughout history seem to have needed religion; and God alone knows what harm (or good) might have flowed if they hadn't found it, in one form or another; human nature being what it is, many people would surely have found other cudgels to wield against their fellows. Stalin, Hitler, and Mao did not call upon any religion to justify their horrendous slaughters; possibly if they'd had a decent faith, they'd have killed fewer people.

Last, and also impossible to quantify, prayers and praise and thanksgiving must benefit many people as they offer them to God. And how much good, if any, do they do for God? Would God like it better if religion did not exist, no one prayed, everyone denied or ignored God, and we took our blessings for granted without ever thanking God? I cannot answer this question, but asking it convinces me further that Dr. Orsi and whoever his like-minded scholars may be indulged in an inevitably ill-founded conclusion. Better, perhaps, if they simply acknowledge the obvious, that much harm has been done in the name of religion.

* * *

Being greedy, vengeful, tough, and so on may have helped our forebears to survive in primitive times long ago or not so long ago; but such behavior is not now a good idea. Jesus, Buddha, Lao Tsu, Confucius, et al. urged us to favor the better angels of our natures. At their best, religions encourage our moral evolution and our most loving, compassionate, constructive selves to prevail over our aggressiveness, greed, anger, vengefulness, and so on. These latter traits may not be entirely evil and may well have been essential for a person or tribe to survive in prehistoric times and sometimes today. While we often use religion to mask (rather than oppose) the degree to which these instincts drive our actions, our better angels must now prevail if we are to survive. At the same time, we need to keep our guard up; peaceful peoples have fallen prey to aggressors. Consider the well-armed but peaceful Swiss and their lofty ally, the Alps.

* * *

A critical task of religion is to move people to stop behaving as "the survival of the fittest" evolved us to behave. So far, religions have done this fairly often among individuals yet failed egregiously to do it among nations, making the Twentieth Century the bloodiest so far. But now technology has exponentially upped the costs and lowered the rewards of war. Perhaps religions will civilize the nations and tribes and powerful assholes before it's too late. Or not.

* * *

A religion's stress, if any, on non-violence seeks the triumph of people's better natures. Yet it's generally acceptable, and a good idea, to use violence to defend ourselves against a violent attack. So attackers, especially aggressor nations, commonly claim that they are acting in self-defense. And America renamed the War Department the Defense Department in 1947-1949 and prefers to call its violence *force*.

* * *

Mainstream clergy and media share conflicting roles: They are expected to tell the truth, yet telling too much truth often land them in trouble. I do wish they'd always tell it anyway.

* * *

Perhaps God looks upon the Earth and sees tribes and churches and nations worshiping God in their different ways, which God always knew would miss the mark by some margin because God chose to remain mysterious. Yet I expect that God also sees that their hearts are in the right place and they are trying their best to get it right—when they are. I hope God smiles upon those who are humble and tolerate diversity, and frowns upon those who stamp out heresy and dissent in the name of God—whose name they are thus taking in vain.

* * *

It behooves religious people to recognize the possibility that some so-called heretics may be closer to the truth than they are—not easy, I expect, for clerics who put received doctrine foremost.

* * *

Wars have been fought and people burned at the stake over points of doctrine. People claiming to know the word of God contradict each other. How does one decide who is correct or closer to the truth? Many answer this question by dismissing doubts and adopting uncritically the whole of the faith they were born into. Since God chooses to remain mysterious throughout this life, I suspect that it does not anger God when people err about God, but that it may grieve God when people use violence to correct or suppress the perceived errors of their fellow humans.

* * *

Calling one myth or another "the Word of God" hangs a "Do Not Disturb" sign on the myth that many of the faithful accept despite all evidence to the contrary. Fortunately, our civilization has progressed to where a dissident's obduracy no longer sparks an auto-da-fé.

* * *

Tolerance: Farheed Zakaria observes that Hindus accept differences that Westerners have fought wars over.[25]

* * *

Honoring diversity: Many devout people hold beliefs and engage in religious practices that I cannot relate to, and, I'm sure, vice versa. I believe this is normal and as it should be.

* * *

Everyone's house is God's house. The great outdoors is God's cathedral.

* * *

People who extol "truth" often fail to tell us what they think their truth consists of.

* * *

Scenario: The more chaotic and perilous that contemporary life becomes, the more pugnaciously people assert questionable religious certainties such as: God wants me to save you my way; an immortal soul enters an ovum the instant a sperm does; God deeded this land to my forebears in perpetuity; and infidel soldiers based on certain soil profane it. Such certainties stoke more chaos and peril, leading to more certainties, and so on down the spiral toilet.

* * *

Various faiths, creeds, denominations, and sects present us with a sweeping package of beliefs, narratives, and commands; and they tell us to accept the whole bundle on pain of spending eternity in hell, or whatever. It's all or nothing. But I cannot blindly believe what I'm told to believe any more than I can love whom I'm told to love, and I suppose this is true for many people who are neither fundamentalists nor wholly intimidated by the threat of damnation that some clerics brandish.

* * *

Martin Luther said that believing and dying are two things we do alone. Yet churches are nothing if not communities of people who are, ipso facto, not alone.

* * *

Some people, I'm told, turn to religion to feel comfortable. While religion does comfort me, that's not why I turn to it. Isn't it religion's business to discomfort us at times? Jesus did. In 2012 Father Roy Bourgeois, whom I consider a hero of the faith, was defrocked (involuntarily laicized) for doing it—for insisting that women should be able to become Catholic priests, which I expect will happen after he and I are long gone.

* * *

Karl Marx famously said that religion is the opium of the people. That may be true for some versions of religion and some passive folks or folks who blandly and maybe blindly accept the status quo. But for many of us, religion stimulates. It may even stimulate heresies.

* * *

As religions evolve, they often tend to make things more complicated than they need to be. Yet rituals and traditions seem to matter, more or less, to zillions of people. Less to Quakers: the closest we come to having sacraments are the marriage ceremony and the memorial service. Yet we have our ways, and some Quakers lord it over others who don't know to follow them.

* * *

The teachings of successful religions seem to strike responsive chords in the best, in That of God or whatever we call it, within large numbers of people who adopt and spread them. Yet a religion of sorts seems to have struck a responsive chord in several hundred people who drank the poison that their charismatic leader told them to at Jonestown in Guyana in 1978. (But note that many of them had to be forced to drink it, and some were shot for refusing to drink it.)

* * *

The fact that the teachings of Jesus resonate within so many of us helps both to explain the popularity of Christianity and to confirm that his main teachings reflect the Word of God. The same holds for the best of other religions. Note how similar many religions are about the best ways to treat our brothers and sisters. Dare I suggest that there was an extra portion of godliness in Jesus, Mohammed, Gautama Buddha, Lao Tzu, Confucius, and others; and that there are many paths to a godly life including a path of atheism?

* * *

I suspect that God is pleased when anyone does God's will, no matter which particular religion, if any, he or she espouses.

* * *

I suspect, too, that the ethics and world view proclaimed by the religions that took hold in Asia—for instance, the Hindu view that life is cyclical, not spiraling upwards—may have resonated within those people much as Christianity has resonated within the Western tradition. Inevitably there is interplay between a culture and the religion(s) it hosts.

* * *

Some versions of religion sugarcoat the harshness of God's creation. Who can deny that many lives are painful and deaths cruel?

* * *

"The common goal of all moral precepts laid down by the great teachers of humanity is unselfishness…. The most important thing is to look at the purpose of religion and not at the details of theology or metaphysics, which can lead to mere intellectualism…. Each religion works in its own way to lessen human suffering and contribute to world civilization. Conversion is not the point…. Rather I try to think of how I as a Buddhist humanitarian can contribute to human happiness…. Each religion has its own distinctive contributions to make, and each in its own way is suitable to a particular group of people as they understand life. The world needs them all."

— His Holiness the Dalai Lama.[26]

* * *

Scholar of religions Karen Armstrong to NPR interviewer Terry Gross on March 8, 2004: The Golden Rule is the essence of religion, whereas belief is a red herring. The test of a belief is whether it leads you to practical compassion. When Rabbi Hillel was asked to recite the Torah, he famously replied, "What is hateful to you do not do to your neighbor. That is the whole Torah. The rest is commentary." Ms. Armstrong seemed to approve. Note that Hillel, whose conclusion I also quote in the Introduction, stated the Golden Rule in the negative, which likely leads to less helping and also less meddling than Jesus's affirmative version: "Therefore whatsoever ye would that men should do to you, do ye even so to them." (Matthew 7:12) Note, too, Hillel's implication that what we do matters more than what we believe.

* * *

Consider, too the Islamic Golden Rule: "None of you truly believes until he wishes for his brother what he wishes for himself."

* * *

Compassion can lead to doing good, though the reverse is not necessarily true. Some people strive to save the world but don't care much for the people in it. Which is too bad but not bad.

* * *

Religions that fail to teach people to be considerate of everyone miss their calling. So do religions that fail to remind us that humility is a seminal virtue that spawns other virtues.

* * *

Both religion and literature may give us the sense that other people are as human and precious as we are. Reading and writing insightful books are religious activities.

* * *

Religions at their best give people a full sense of the humanity of all people, as do the great novels. Purportedly religious actions that flout people's humanity—for instance, the Crusades, the tortures of the Inquisition, wars over doctrine, and the bellicose rants of some clerics today—are wolves in the clothing of the Lamb.

* * *

The myths of the major religions differ from each other far more than their insights into compassionate conduct, that is, what doesn't matter differs far more than what does. I suspect this is as God would have it.

* * *

The closer the several faiths come to stating God's truth, the more closely they resemble each other. They form a pyramid of sorts, widely separate at the base by their differing histories, mythologies, and rituals, yet converging ever closer as they reach their apex. Scholar of religions Karen Armstrong writes that, "All the world faiths claim that compassion is...the prime virtue and true test of religiosity...." I believe that compassion tips the peak of the pyramid.[ix]

---

ix Ms. Armstrong's Charter for Compassion is printed in Appendix A.

The Bible

Our acceptance of the Scriptures actually depends, not upon our faith in God, but upon our faith in the men (always men, I'm told) who wrote them down, decided to include them in the canon, copied them, copied the copies, ventured minor edits, and translated. If God had inspired the information about physics, geology, and so on that is written or implicit in the Bible, one assumes that God would have gotten it right. I have faith that the godliness of those men inspired much of their wisdom and many of their choices, though not all.

* * *

I refer herein to *Scriptures* without differentiating between the Hebrew Bible (Old Testament) and New Testament whenever I think my thought applies to both, which is usually.

* * *

Behind the Scriptures included in the Bible stand many more writings from which they were chosen and hence many decisions about which to include and omit. Were the men who made these selections always divinely inspired? Were none of the rejected texts divinely inspired? And what inspired the copiers who, by error or intention, changed the texts?

* * *

Believing as I do that the echo of God in each of us opens us to receiving divine revelation, I suppose that the men who created much of the Bible were similarly open, perhaps more than most of us. So which, if any, passages embody divine revelation and which don't?

* * *

Many who (unlike Quakers) believe that divine revelation stopped with the completion of the New Testament frequently come upon new revelation that they call "interpretation."

* * *

The Bible was written by people who apparently had much faith and knew much about human nature but relatively little about the cosmos and the wonders that God wrought in creating it. They presumably did their best to figure it all out, which was understandable; but claiming that their writings are the perfect and immutable word of God has led to trouble.

* * *

"Creation myth" is what we call every other culture's explanation for how the world and people came into being, but, *mirabile dictu,* the explanation in Genesis is divinely accurate.

* * *

The echo of God within the people who wrote, edited, selected, and copied the Scriptures may have helped to keep them on track in the face of their inevitable biases, assumptions, agendas, culture, and perhaps external pressures. But surely not perfectly.

* * *

Our need to decide what writings in the Bible to reject arises from the fact that the people who created it decided what parts to include. Sometimes rightly and sometimes wrongly I suppose, they took those risks; and they presumed—or others presumed for them or after them—that they were recording God's truth. It was their presumption that created our need to presume to judge what to accept and reject and wonder about. Most of us don't have schooling that would help, but I believe that all of us have the still, small voice.

* * *

Of all the Biblical myths, the overriding myth is the claim that the whole book was divinely inspired. For many, the book is a key source of wisdom and inspiration, but it alienates many others who focus on its errors and contradictions; so they abandon religion, throwing out the baby with the bath water, heedless that much of the Bible is wonderfully sound and merits their attention.

* * *

It saddened me to learn, correctly I think, that the magnificent prose of the King James Version was based in good part on a flawed translation. I have tried to take the passages of Scripture quoted in this book from the KJV whenever they are readily comprehensible and accord with a translation that is based on careful scholarship.

* * *

It's best not to dwell on, or feel guilty about, passages of the Bible that we find hard to accept. "Jesus walked on water." At the same time, we need the humility to learn from Scriptures to break out of our complacency and improve our conduct. "Turn the other cheek." But which Scriptures? The key writings of any religion, I suppose, are those that strike responsive chords in our hearts, reflect our own best self (Inward Light), move us to act compassionately towards others, and bring peace to them and within ourselves.

* * *

It is widely recognized that the Bible contradicts itself, makes statements that are mutually exclusive or have been proved not to have happened, and, crucially, that go against the spirit of what it tells us Jesus meant. So I take personal responsibility for choosing what I accept, question, and reject, guided by the wisdom of others and my too fallible, inevitably biased guidance from whatever godliness resides within me. I do the best I can, certain only that I cannot be certain and will sometimes err though I won't know when—until maybe later. Fortunately, the passages that advise us how to treat other people matter most and seem generally sound.

* * *

If Divine inspiration does not err, then the stuff the Bible got wrong was not divinely inspired.

* * *

Trial lawyers love to catch a witness in a lie and use that one lie—the more glaring, the better—to convince the jury to disbelieve everything else that this "untrustworthy" person says. The tactic often works. Unfortunately, some people, wittingly or not, impose a similar test on the Bible. They perceive one or more errors; then, sometimes sadly, sometimes gleefully, they go on to disbelieve it all. This is their great error.

* * *

Experienced lawyers, myself included, soundly question the credibility of witnesses who claim to be repeating the precise words of long vanished conversations. The Gospel of John is replete with such words. Yet the dubious credibility of these verbatim quotations need not divert us from the messages they seek to convey.

* * *

Ernest Hemingway said that a good writer needs "a built-in, shock-proof, shit detector." The same holds for readers of the Bible. Were all its authors, committees, editors, copiers, and translators divinely inspired at all pertinent times? Our common sense, knowledge of scientific discoveries, and sporadic capacity to feel Scriptures resonate may constitute our detector, giving us guidance that is not perfect—but then, neither were the authors of the Bible. Presumably most of them and most of us have done the best we could.

* * *

Re the fact that Gospels of Matthew, Luke, and John report sayings and doings of Jesus that the first-written Mark does not: Some scholars assure us that various motives, agendas, and biases led the later writers to record and maybe slant or invent certain of Jesus' words and deeds. Maybe so, at least in part, but it doesn't seem to occur to these scholars that a significant motive may simply have been that Mark's brief version omitted words and deeds of Jesus that the later writers considered worth reporting.

* * *

A venerable and useful approach to Scripture is to ask: What does it say? What does it mean? What does it mean for me? And not to forget: What, if anything, ought I to do about it?

* * *

The Scriptures say what they say, or do they? In the 1980s, Nancy and I were part of a group of Quakers that drew meanings from several Gospel passages that were entirely different from the meanings drawn from the same passages by a group of *campesinos* in Solentiname, Nicaragua, who were trying to cope with the violent Somoza dictatorship of the 1970s.[27] To some extent, the Scriptures are a Rorschach, an inkblot test. That of God or of Satan or of whatever in readers—and certainly readers' biases, anxieties, and life experiences—informs the various meanings they draw from the same texts.

* * *

Some highlights of the Bible tell us how to behave: The Ten Commandments. Love God with all one's heart and one's neighbor as one's self. Do justice, love mercy and walk humbly with our God. Forgive seventy times seven (= 490 times, an example perhaps of Jesus's use of hyperbole to impress a point). Do unto others as you would have them do unto you. "Inasmuch as ye have done it unto one of the least of these my brethren, ye have done it unto me." (Matthew 25:40) For me, such passages are the easiest to trust and matter the most.

* * *

One evening in June 2015, a young white man named Dylan Roof joined a

Bible study group in a church in Charleston, South Carolina, sat amongst the Black parishioners for a time, then pulled out a pistol, and shot nine of them dead. A number of loved ones of the people he killed forgave Roof and prayed for his soul. Later a federal court sentenced him to be executed, and a state court, to serve life without parole. I admire the people who forgave Roof and agree with the state court's sentence. Forgiving his deeds does not cancel the need to punish him, put him safely away, and make an example of him—an example to show thoughtless people how terribly wrong he was.

* * *

The Commandment against making graven images means for me: Don't elevate fancy autos or boats or jewelry and so on into objects of pressing importance. Recall how Dutch people of long ago elevated tulips. So don't fritter away our gift of life at that level of triviality.

* * *

Focusing on niceties of Biblical interpretation may divert, though not excuse, one from doing what matters.

* * *

Undue concern and discussion have been focused upon the minutiae of the Scriptures. Realizing that many passages are not accurately rendered[28] may (or may not) help us to see that we do better to focus more on the big, simple, irrefutably accurate and sound lessons. Many Quakers, for instance, try to do this by living out our testimonies of peace, equality, integrity, simplicity, and so on, which are not free-floating creations but emanate from Scripture.

* * *

The symbolism, numerology, lineage, predictions, and fulfillments of prophecies that appear in the Scriptures may be invoked to demonstrate authority, authoritativeness, or some other point. But they have, at best, little bearing on how we treat people.

* * *

The proof of the pudding is in the eating. The proof of the Gospels is in living them now.

* * *

"The miracle of the Bible is the way in which it helps to interpret our experiences, and the way in which our experiences help us to interpret it."
— Reverend William Howard Melish in 1953[29]

Jews

Jews are plainly a chosen people of God to the extent that they have shepherded the three great monotheistic religions into the world, and all three go back to Father Abraham. Yet I cannot believe that God values the life of a Jew any more or less than the life of a Christian, Muslim, atheist, or of an Anglo-Irishman like me. Is the life of a Jew inherently more precious to God than that of an Australian Aborigine?

* * *

I cannot believe that a God who loves everybody would forever favor any one group—Jews, Evangelicals, or anyone else—to the exclusion of the rest of humankind, comfortable and common as it is for many peoples to assure themselves that they are God's favorites. But by the ways that the Jews chose to worship God and venerate their book about God and all that flowed from those choices, they elevated themselves—which may have been God's way of choosing them through their own free will.

* * *

So far as I have discerned, Jesus was the prime vehicle for God's truth, the chosen person among a chosen people who don't believe that God chose him. That is their choice, and I would not fault them for theirs any more than I want them to fault me for mine.

* * *

We are taught that Jews were God's chosen people and that God chose a Jew to be Jesus's mother. As and when the Word became flesh, it was the flesh of a Middle-Eastern Jew. Anti-Semitism is not only unchristian but, for Christians, an absurd contradiction.

* * *

Ancient Hebrews struggled to praise the God whom words cannot describe. Since Hitler, Jews have struggled to condemn the crime that words cannot describe. Jews bear the glory and the burden of being a chosen people, but the glory was earned and the burden was not. It is an astounding shame that many Christians have been so unchristian as to assail the people who wrote the book that underlies their faith and birthed and taught their Savior, who was steeped in Judaism and called "rabbi." How presumptuous to attack God's chosen people! Or to attack any people!

* * *

The Hebrew Bible teaches that God chose the Hebrews; and a recurring question for them then and for everyone today is, Shall we choose God?

* * *

I believe that being a chosen people has limits and that God also loves people who are neither Jews nor Catholics nor Muslims nor evangelical Christians, and so on; in short, that God loves everybody.

* * *

Whether or not the God of all the cosmos once parceled out any piece of Middle Eastern real estate to one tribe or another, I would think that God's greater concern is for all of God's peoples to live at peace and with respect, or at least tolerance, for each other, whatever their history and wherever they dwell.

* * *

Every time I think about what the Nazis and other Europeans who were homicidally hostile towards Jews would have done to my precious daughter and granddaughters who are Jews, my commitment to non-violence and the Quaker peace testimony fades away, and I seethe with anger. Progeny aside, if I had been a Quaker and a few years older during World War II, I would have been among the many Quakers who joined the military to stop the Nazis. (More on this at pp. 165) Thus, violence begets violence, even in many like me who normally abjure it.

Isaac

Abraham, we are told, reached the point of sacrificing the life of his son Isaac because he perceived that God was telling him to. Fortunately for Isaac, Abraham, and future Jews, God spared Isaac at the last moment, and Abraham slew a handy ram instead. (Genesis 22:1-14) What can we say for a God who would order a man to sacrifice his child? Or for a father who would obey it? Or for generations of Jews and Christians who have venerated this story of such a man's devotion to such a God? Or for me who did not think to ask these questions until I was old? This God of fatal testing looks insecure and has reportedly admitted to being jealous. (Exodus 20:5) The God that I believe in is larger than that. My God rewards belief but does not demand loyalty to the point of committing murder, nor of traumatizing a boy with terror, nor of horrifying a mother and stressing a marriage, in order to test a fathers' devotion to the Great Mystery or to a voice inside his head.

The story of the so-called Binding of Isaac has apparently troubled many people for millennia, and rightly so. It may show Abraham as being faithful to a fault, but what does it say about God? What did God gain putting Abraham to such a test? Some of today's street gangs make new members prove their loyalty by killing a person. Is God no better than those gangs?

Some learned people say that God never intended that Abraham would sacrifice Isaac. How do *they* know what God intended? From Isaac's perspective, his dad performed a mock execution. Until Isaac realized he was still alive, he was probably scared shitless. How could he love such a dad after that? How long, if ever, did it take him to forgive him? Mock executions of suspected terrorists by the CIA, among many others, are rightly considered torture. What kind of a God would put a father and son—and mother when she found out—through *that*?

Others say that Abraham was actually testing God, pretending to go ahead with the blood sacrifice until God stopped him—playing chicken with God, as it were. How presumptuous would Abraham have been to test the Creator of the cosmos? Still others say that Abraham went along with God's directions because he had faith that God would stop him in time. Or that God simply wanted Abraham to play catch-and-release with Isaac, and Abraham mistakenly thought that God was telling him to actually kill the lad. Again, this is guesswork, reading stuff into the text that contradicts the actual words in order to make God and Abraham look less horrid, even though many of these interpreters also believe that the text records the words of God. These words say what God said and didn't say. Does fairly interpreting the story permit cleaning it up by adding stuff that isn't in it?

Rabbi Harold Kushner, who is probably best known for his book *When Bad Things Happen to Good People*, calls the Binding of Isaac "the single most enigmatic story in the entire Torah.... I have consulted every commentary I could find... [and] I never found an interpretation that made sense of it or that left me able to admire either God for making the demand or Abraham for being so ready to obey it." Finally, though, Rabbi Kushner found an interpretation that he could favor, namely, that "Abraham trusted God to keep His promise to make him the progenitor of a great nation.... He relied on God to intervene at the last moment so that God's promise of progeny would not be thwarted."[30]

Does this interpretation read in things that aren't there? Note that Isaac's seed was not the only means by which God could have kept the promise to Abraham. He had already fathered Ishmael by Hagar, and Almighty God could surely have arranged for Abraham to have enough lead in his pencil to sire other children.

I told my son Brian that if God ever instructed me to sacrifice him, I'd tell that God to stuff it. Brian said he was glad to hear it.

Did the Binding of Isaac really happen? I doubt it. Whether it did or not, why was a story included in the Scriptures that casts God and the forefather of the Jews in such a bad light? Same question re all the horrors that God is said to have inflicted on Job to test Job's faithfulness. I cannot second-guess the priorities of the guys who wrote those Scriptures millennia ago, but I can and do reject the needlessly petty and cruel image of God that they expounded. God may have sacrificed zillions lives in the process of evolution, but that was in a useful cause. Since a happy result was the creation of us humans, we would be ungrateful to complain too loudly.

Consider how the story fits the present. How many parents have sacrificed their sons on orders from the draft board or by urging them to enlist? The Binding of Isaac has been called, soundly I believe, a metaphor for our culture's tradition of fathers and mothers sending their sons off to be killed in one war or another. Leonard Cohen explained that he intended his haunting song "Story of Isaac" (1969) to be more than simply an anti-war protest, because, he said, "Human beings being what they are, we're always going to set up people to die for some absurd situation that we define as important."[31]

Jesus

Is Jesus the human face of God? Does he bring humanity to the Mystery? He is surely a bridge between God and vast numbers of people. He taught that God cares about everyone and it's best if we do too. He risked his life and lost it in order to spread his message of forgiveness, peace, inclusion, and compassion. For me, the accounts of his parentage, miracles, resurrection, and precise relationship to God have little bearing on the ways he taught us to live a godly life.

* * *

I believe that the Holy Spirit suffused the man Jesus, though not completely since he sometimes got stuff wrong—the imminent end of humankind, for instance.

* * *

If Jesus was co-equal with God, why did he sometimes get his facts and predictions wrong? Could all of them have been errors by the Gospel writers and copiers?

* * *

Jesus was clearly inspired by God and perhaps sent by God; but unlike so many of the faithful, I do not see him as being a part of God, or God come to Earth in human form. For me, he was the greatest of the prophets. A billion or so Muslims claim the same for Mohammed. Though Jesus was reportedly combative on occasion, I prize him as the Prince of Peace.

* * *

To follow Jesus does not mean to become an itinerant preacher, nor to swear fealty to him, nor to believe everything he is said to have said and done. For me, it means to let his words and example inform the ways we choose to live and speak and treat others. If that sounds dull, recall that Jesus often partied.

* * *

Perhaps wishfully, I picture Jesus as being compassionate, convivial, learned in the Hebrew Scriptures, exceptionally wise, charismatic, a powerful speaker, strong enough to upset the moneychangers' tables in the Temple, and having brown eyes and features that would fit in with a group of his fellow Middle Easterners—not the face of the white, uncrowned King Arthur that we see in a standard picture of him—in all, an outstanding human being. Americans of both sexes might note that Jesus managed to be a mensch without being macho.

* * *

I expect that Mary conceived Jesus with the Holy Spirit perhaps and surely with Joseph in the usual way. Not that this matters to me, except that exalting a virgin birth (as several faiths claim for their founders) diminishes God's gift of procreation by the carnal and often loving coupling of a woman and a man.

* * *

The line in "Away in a Manger" that says "little Lord Jesus, no crying he makes" was presumably meant to suggest that Jesus was perfect from birth. But if he didn't cry, how was Mary to know when to offer the tiny tyke her breast or change his nappy? If the baby never cries, call the doctor! The lyrics typify the treacle that clutters much Christian tradition, suggesting as it does a preference for fantasy over God's world as it is.

* * *

Whether or not God was Jesus's "birth father," it seems clear that Joseph was the father and Mary the mother who reared him. That Jesus turned out so well must, in part at least, be thanks to these earthly parents whom, we are told, God chose for the job.

* * *

"For ye have the poor always with you," said Jesus (Matthew 26:11); and Jesus kept company with the poor and prostitutes and tax collectors, and not with the crowd that lounged around the heated swimming pool at the Roman Embassy in Jerusalem.

* * *

One day when my friend Sean Dougherty was sitting beside an elderly woman named Violeta during a mass in Cuernavaca, Mexico, the Gospel reading was the Beatitudes. (Matthew 5: 3-13) Sean asked Violeta afterwards what she thought Jesus meant by, "Blessed are the poor."

"I don't know," she said, "but I think it means that we hold a special place in his heart."

Sean asked her why the poor would be special for Jesus, and she replied,

"I think it is because we are the ones who listen to him."[x]

* * *

In the stories of the healing miracles, Jesus says repeatedly that the person's own faith caused the healing. We may doubt, if we wish, that all those people were actually healed; but to the extent that they were, it seems likely that, as Jesus said, their faith was therapeutic. But anyone he reportedly revived from the dead was presumably beyond having faith, and I have to doubt that he reversed the decomposition of any cadaver.

* * *

When my son Brian arrived during the end of a thunderstorm in July 1965, I was able to be present during his birth, though in those days most fathers were not. "It really is a miracle," I told the veteran obstetrician.

"Yes," he said, "it really is."

What gives me hope is less the reports that Jesus arose from the dead than the commonplace miracle that babies constantly emerge into new life from their mothers' wombs.

* * *

If the words and example of Jesus had not resonated within his followers, he would almost certainly have been soon forgotten. It's problematic, though, that false prophets, too, may strike responsive chords in many people, and faux faiths result—though few seem to survive the test of time.

* * *

During a group discussion at a Priory retreat in March of 2006, Kevin Kelly, who was once a priest, said, "The God in me responds to the God in you." I agreed and was prompted to think that the God within many millions has responded to the God within Jesus. Were it not so, Christianity would not have survived and flourished through the centuries.

(Please note that the brothers whom I cite from time to time are the Benedictine monks of the Weston Priory in Weston, Vermont. The lay people—Kevin, Jerry, Delores, et al.—are friends of the brothers and of Nancy and me. Listening to and talking with these people during twenty-five or so years helped in shaping my views. My heresies are probably my own.)

* * *

---

x Sean Dougherty is Executive Director of VAMOS! (Vermont Associates for Mexican Opportunity and Support!), a small non-profit that provides meals, education, and basic medical and dental care to about 750 impoverished youngsters and 200 of their mothers in and around Cuernavaca, Mexico. Nancy and I served on the VAMOS! Board.

Jerry Richard, a retired schoolteacher, said he believed that Jesus was divine but no more so than anyone else. I agree to the extent of accepting the Quaker belief that there is That of God in everyone—though the best part of Jesus constituted a far larger portion of his being, I'm sure, than the best part of me does of mine.

* * *

Was Jesus divine? Aren't we all? Wasn't Jesus more so? I'm sure he was, but there are questions of greater moment.

* * *

If Jesus had been a non-violent Quaker, would he have upset the tables of the money-changers in the Temple (Matt. 21:12)?

* * *

Jesus sought to be a religious reformer. As did Martin Luther in 1517. As did George Fox in 1652 for us Quakers. But Jesus was so much more.

* * *

"I believe in...one Lord Jesus Christ, the only-begotten Son of God; Begotten of his Father before all worlds, God of God...Being of one substance with the Father...." So says the Nicene Creed as printed in *The Book of Common Prayer*.[32] A great many followers of Jesus call him God's only son and elevate him to equality with God as part of a Trinity of Father, Son, and Holy Spirit. Followers of Buddha, Mohammed, Lao Tzu, and Confucius, on the other hand, consider that these founders were exalted prophets but not co-equal or co-eternal with an Almighty. Though I cannot be certain that Jesus was not all that his most ardent followers say he was, it's my belief that he was an exalted prophet and perhaps more godly than the other great prophets, and that any such comparisons have no bearing on the truth of his message and theirs.

* * *

If I understand correctly, many Christians believe that Jesus was actually God, or an aspect of God, inhabiting the body of a man, dying the death of a man, and arising from death to sit, at least figuratively, at the right hand of God or another aspect of God. It strikes me as a bit much to suggest that any human being could be co-equal with the Creator of this magnificent cosmos and all that's in it. The men who long ago elevated Jesus to that exalted status thought that this tiny Earth lay at the heart of all Creation and had existed for only a few thousand years; they did not have a clue about all that it took to create it. Thus, making this claim for Jesus back then was less grandiose than it may seem today.

* * *

Re Quakers' lack of a formal creed: I dare say that most Catholics' and Protestants' belief about whether Jesus was always God's son or was simply a man inspired by God or had some other relationship to God has little bearing on how ready they are to forgive those who trespass against them.

* * *

Science has determined that the Big Bang (or whatever started the current edition of Creation) occurred about 13.8 billion years ago. If Jesus were co-eternal with God, he, too, must have existed in some form before that event. This sounds unlikely. He was a man, and men evolved only recently. What would Jesus have been doing during all those eons before Mary bore him into human life? He could not have visited other planets during the billions of years before there were any. In other words, scientific discovery casts further doubt on the dogma that Jesus and God are co-eternal. Not that the accuracy of the dogma affects the godliness of Jesus's teachings.

The above assumes that time and space as we know them are the reality in which God and Jesus have existed. But if there is also a timeless reality, Jesus might have existed in it before he was born on Earth. Perhaps as the opening of the Gospel of John suggests, he existed as the Word. But what does the Word mean?

* * *

If there is a Trinity, do its three beings have separate intelligences? Do they talk to each other and occasionally disagree and argue? Or get pissed off at each other? Do the Father and Son avoid the common disputes between fathers and sons? I suppose that when Jesus walked the Earth and talked with God, his intelligence was separate from God's. If he shared God's presumed knowledge of the future, did he understand throughout his ministry, and even his childhood, that he would be tortured to death?

We read that Jesus called out from his lonely wooden tower (as Leonard Cohen put it), "My God. My God. Why hast thou forsaken me?" Is this a question that God would ask God?

My own conclusion is that the Holy Spirit is an aspect of God that suffused the man Jesus to an unusual degree—as it probably filled Mohammed, Buddha, Lao Tzu, and the founders of some other religions. Is this sufficient?

* * *

As to the idea of a Trinity, there is for me one God, manifested in many ways. Jesus was, so far as I know, God's best though imperfect human messenger.

* * *

According to the Koran, "people who say that God is the third of three are defying [the truth]; there is only one God," while Jesus "was only a messenger." Pope Francis, on the other hand, has said that Trinitarianism should be treated as a monotheistic belief.[33] If his view holds, fine. If not, the difference doesn't strike me as something God wants people to fight over.

* * *

My friend Don Conover says that the arrival of Jesus was a clear intervention in the world by God.

* * *

If the words and example of Jesus taught us a good portion of God's will, then what does it matter whether Jesus performed any or all of the miracles that the Gospels attribute to him or fulfilled previous prophesies or was God's only son or his mother was a virgin, or even whether he vanished from the tomb and arose from the dead? Likewise, if his words and deeds do not teach God's will, what does the rest of it matter?

* * *

If Jesus had taught that we should hate our neighbors, would any miracles he performed or his relationship to God or his reported after-death appearances validate that teaching? How do we know that such a teaching would have been ungodly? By common sense? Because it clashes with Jesus's other teachings? Or clashes with the godliness within us? Or all of the above?

* * *

If the Son had taught us to hate our enemies, then many would probably trust that such a teaching must be godly. Such is the power of authority. And the need to think for ourselves.

* * *

Jesus's close relationship to God appears less from the bare words of his teachings than from the godliness that we may recognize in his teachings, example, and sacrifice. How did we acquire (who gave us) the ability to recognize godliness? Is our recognition of it always true?

* * *

The Gospels report that Jesus stressed faith and belief, but a fairly simple faith and belief, for instance, faith in God and God's power flowing through him to cure illness, restore eyesight, drive out demons—not a faith in doctrines that some faithful people constructed and others killed each other over long afterwards. Of greater moment for me, Jesus laid great stress on deeds, on loving God and our neighbors (which are deeds), feeding the hungry, clothing the naked, and visiting the sick and imprisoned. Jesus is also said to have said that those who don't do these compassionate deeds enter into "everlasting punishment." (Matthew 25: 31-46) Punishment in Hell? Or imprisonment in one's self-absorbed self?

* * *

Jesus was martyred for his words and example, for the sake of his followers, and ultimately for all humankind, whereas no one executed Buddha, Mohammed, Lao Tzu, or Confucius. Consider that these other prophets inspired vast followings by what they taught—all without performing miracles, being martyred, or arising from the dead.

* * *

Jesus helped folks to prepare for eternity, not by dying for our alleged sins, but by helping us to be the better people on Earth that I believe we shall continue to be in an afterlife.

* * *

How did the physical sacrifice of a prophet, however exalted, cancel zillions of unborn people's alleged sins? How does his sacrifice credibly connect to other people's sins at all? I'm not arguing that these questions don't have answers.

* * *

Everyone has a lower nature that is greedy, violent, and vengeful, and a higher nature that is generous, peaceful, and forgiving. Jesus is a savior or redeemer at least to the extent that he showed us that it's God's way for us to follow our higher (more godly) natures. He, Saint Paul, and his other followers made it respectable and desirable to do this, and so to lead the more fulfilled lives that result. But his words and example challenged and offended the Establishment of his day (and much of ours) so much that they crucified him then and widely ignore his message now—often behind a facade of church-going, word-mouthing, charity-giving piety. He gave up his life, I think, not for our alleged sin-from-birth or the sin of the mythical Adam and Eve, but in an effort to save us from our propensity to do harm and fail to do good—as many before and after him have given their lives, some by tortures maybe more agonizing than crucifixion—there weren't any electrodes in those days—to help people in need.

* * *

Redemption: Did Jesus, by dying as he did in a little corner of the Middle East, redeem the alleged sins of vast numbers of people yet unborn? Many Christians say so. It is clear to me that Jesus gave his life for the sake of humankind in that he understood his words and deeds would get him killed, yet he went ahead so as to help us to lead more godly and fulfilled lives.

* * *

A great many people acknowledge or claim Jesus as the savior of their souls but fail to live as he taught. Through sophistry or thoughtlessness or whatever, they tend to follow their lower natures at the expense of their higher natures, pursue selfish interests at the expense of their fellows, and put themselves, more or less, on the wrong side of Jesus's parable of the sheep and the goats (again, Matthew 25:31-46). Piety alone does not suffice. Piety masks many sins.

* * *

Whether the wine at a Eucharist is the blood of Jesus which was shed for us, or a symbol or reminder of his blood, what difference does drinking it make an hour later when another driver infuriates us by taking the parking space that we had our eye on at the Mall?

* * *

The fact that other religions hold much in common with Christianity shows that God has spoken through more people than Jesus, the Hebrew prophets, and the writers of the Bible. For example, through Mohammed. As a Quaker, I believe that God spoke some words through our founder, George Fox, during the 17th Century and may speak a word or two through you and me.

* * *

Jesus did not preach needed social changes *per se*, but the logical conclusion of what he did preach leads thoughtful people towards them. Consider the Catholic teachings on economic justice that began in modern times with Pope Leo XIII's 1891 encyclical *Rerum Novarum* and have been amplified by more recent papal declarations. (More on this at pp. 167–168 below.) Whether as a result of these teachings or other faith-based initiatives or simple human decency, the march towards fair wages, workplace safety, universal health care, and so on has advanced nicely in much of Europe, in the U.S. not so much.

* * *

Did Jesus fail to understand the full implications of his message, for example, that slavery was unchristian? Or did he perhaps realize that if he denounced slavery, he would be killed before he could deliver his main messages? He showed as little interest in social reform as in driving the Romans from his homeland. Rather, he pursued the far broader goal of softening people's hearts and elevating their conduct, which his true followers pursue today.

* * *

Salvation: I believe that Jesus died, not to absolve our sins in some mystical way, but as a price he willingly paid in order to show his followers how to lead richer, less sinful (hurtful), more peaceful and godly lives, and in *that* sense to be saved. He must have known that agonizing death awaited him if he persisted, yet he persisted all the same. For us. Thank you, Jesus.

* * *

Did Jesus redeem us from our sins or from Original Sin by taking them or it upon himself? I don't think so—nor that we enter the world under a burden of sin in the first place—though of course I could be wrong. How does an innocent man take on another person's sin as though it were a backpack?

* * *

A challenge that Jesus faced: To speak the word of God from a backwater of the Roman Empire, yet not get himself killed before he got going. As it was, it wasn't far into his ministry that the Establishment of that time and place rid themselves of him—or so they thought. For they soon vanished into the dustbin of history but he lives in more hearts today than any other person.

* * *

Jesus had to eschew politics if he was to spread his message. Many of his current followers feel they need to involve themselves in politics if they are to follow his message. Therein lie many opportunities and problems. Starting with many people's refusal to see that the same deed can be both political and religious.

* * *

Though not overtly a political revolutionary or social reformer, Jesus challenged the System and paid the price.

* * *

"They killed Jesus because he had a big mouth."
                                    — Our friend Delores Barbeau, February 2012.

* * *

It's well that Jesus spoke in parables and other indirection, for if he had been more overtly revolutionary, the Establishment would have eliminated him sooner; we would know little or nothing about him; and there would be no Christianity. But as if someone had planned it, and certainly as St. Paul and others assisted it, Christianity became the dominant religion of the Roman Empire, the U.S. Empire, and others in between. Not that the masters of these empires have practiced Christianity as Jesus intended it, but many commoners have.

* * *

For years I wondered why Jesus would admonish people not to tell anyone about one or another of his good deeds. Then I learned that the CIA-advised Guatemalan army of the 1970s and 1980s often assassinated the local leaders in Mayan villages. Nothing personal, they simply wanted to keep the people leaderless. The logic of military dictatorships must be fairly constant through the ages. So perhaps Jesus did not want to be seen as a leader or outstanding person and thus attract the fatal attention of the Roman rulers before he was well into his ministry.

* * *

The Trojan horse of Jesus's ambiguity: By casting his revolutionary message in comparatively non-threatening terms, he opened Rome and later empires to accepting Christianity. But trying to advance the equality and compassion that are at the heart of Christianity remains a constant struggle; equality has never prevailed, and peace is random.

* * *

The old, destructive debate over whether it was *the* Jews or *the* Romans who killed Jesus could not exist without an obtuse failure of intelligence. It was actually a few of each, while the vast majority of Jews and Romans had nothing to do with it. Italians, although progeny of the Romans, were not demonized as "Christ killers," but became leaders of his church. But Jews....

* * *

When Jesus gave us the Beatitude, "Blessed are the meek for they shall inherit the earth" (Matthew 5:5), he may have been predicting the advent of an economy that is far more equitable than today's frequent push to exploit the meek: To sell them a house they can't afford and a new car before they need one. To con them into voting for candidates who will sell them out and rip them off. Incidentally, I would prefer a translation that says, "Blessed are the humble."

* * *

Brother John: "Knowing all the answers is not the same as knowing the truth." It was given to Jesus, not to know all the answers—he was as bound as other mortals by much of the ignorance of his day, erroneously asserting, for instance, that the end of the world was near—but to know, preach, and live crucial parts of God's truth. But not all God's truth, much of which has been revealed to the prophets of other faiths and is being revealed today.

* * *

Brother Mark said that when we do as Jesus taught, live his way, and act on his behalf, we resurrect him.

* * *

Christians call Jesus God's only son. But perhaps God sent a daughter; and since she was a woman, the people of that day and place did not heed her. Today many people are heeding God's daughters. Though the men who run the Catholic Church have yet to ordain them priests.

And perhaps God sent another son or daughter who spoke out for social and economic justice, and the Establishment dispatched him or her before she or he could win a broad enough following to spark inconvenient reforms.

* * *

Does God send a Jesus to every planet that produces humans or some equivalent beings? Or is Earth—which obviously needed a Jesus and a Mohammed and a Buddha and so on—the only planet that has received them? I once asked this question to a priest in the Anglican tradition of the Church of Ireland. He replied that it would depend on whether those beings on other planets were in need of salvation. I agreed, though I suspect that we saw *salvation* differently.

* * *

There are points at which we may choose to be true to either the spirit of Jesus as we perceive it or to literal words attributed to him that conflict with his spirit. For me, being faithful to Jesus requires being unfaithful to parts of Scripture, which many call the Word of God.

* * *

Much as I admire many Christians who keep Jesus central in their lives, I do not join them. Actually, I admire the people of any faith who take their faith seriously, except those—Muslim terrorists, Catholic sexists, some Quakers, everyone who says you must do it my way—whose faith or distortion of faith leads them to hurt people.

* * *

Much like the Bible as a whole, Jesus presents a Rorschach test, in that people may read things into his life and words that reflect their needs, anxieties, and desires more than his purposes. These subjective readings seem inevitable and may often be sound.

* * *

A view that echoed in the 1962-1965 Vatican II conferences under the now-sainted Pope John XXIII: The truth of God is present in many who never heard of Jesus.

* * *

The final word is never spoken. People today are augmenting and adapting the messages of Jesus and other prophets to the ever-changing present. Why would God want it otherwise in evolving societies on an evolving planet?

Judas

As I understand the history, the local Establishment was certain to eliminate Jesus, the holy troublemaker, whether or not Judas betrayed him. Judas, heinous as his betrayal was, was not essential to the crucifixion and all that followed, though he may have hastened them a bit.

Peter

"And he said, I tell thee, Peter, the cock shall not crow this day, before that thou shalt thrice deny that thou knowest me." (Luke 22:54-62) Of course Peter did deny knowing Jesus as Jesus had predicted; and following the stance of the Gospels, Christians have criticized Peter for these denials ever since. But perhaps a Guatemalan named Antonio sheds a different light on Peter's choices, as he tells us how he and his father managed to save him from an agonizing death at the hands of the secret police in Guatemala City in 1981. Here is Antonio's account:

"Four men in plain clothes with the machine guns and .45 caliber pistols came into my father's office. I was among a group of several young men that were in the hall, and we could hear and see everything that was happening in the office. The men showed my father a composite picture of my family. My father looked at it and said, 'Looks like me, doesn't it?' They asked him some more questions, and then they told him, 'This morning when you left the house, there was another man with you. Where is that man?' My father said, 'It was my son Antonio, but I dropped him off at the bus station. He's there picking up my daughter Adriana, who is coming from Jutiapa.' It wasn't true. I was in the hall. Then they said, 'You have to accompany us.' My father said, 'Okay, just let me put my jacket on.' And my father not even once turned around to look at me. He put his jacket on and left without even looking at me. They left the building, and I with the other men came to the door, and we saw that the cars were heading in the direction of downtown, two cars with no license plates.

"Adriana and I never saw our father again. He was almost certainly tortured to death, as I would have been if I had acknowledged him and been arrested too. For what? By silently denying my father, I survived to tell Adriana how our father was 'disappeared,' then to escape to Mexico and lead a fairly normal life as an exile from the terror in my homeland."[xi]

---

xi I relate this event as Antonio told it to his sister Adriana and she told it to me. I am writing a book called *Sisters in the Storm* about Adriana and two other valiant women who challenged the U.S.-backed Guatemalan security forces in the 1980s and 1990s. Adriana's account of her brother's escape and their father's capture is taken from that book.

I think it was not shameful, but prudent and in furtherance of God's purpose, for Peter to deny Jesus. Acknowledging him at that point could not have saved him, but could easily have cost Peter his own life too. Then who would have founded the Church? Anyone? Any better?

Faulting Peter for his alleged betrayal of Jesus is in the venerable tradition of seeking to appear pure by sacrificing what is useful—being faithful to the point of hurting the cause. By saving his own life that night, Peter was able to become more faithful than if he had sacrificed it in the glorious but futile gesture of getting himself nailed to a cross beside Jesus.

I can imagine Jesus saying to himself as he was being arrested, "For God's sake, Peter, don't acknowledge me. Don't give yourself away, get yourself busted, and sacrifice the good work you still need to do."

* * *

Similarly, a woman named Rufina Amaya hid in the bushes while her child and all her friends and neighbors—more than eight hundred of them—were being massacred by the U.S.-advised Atlacatl Battalion in and near the village of El Mozote in El Salvador in 1981. Those who fault Peter or Antonio may also fault Rufina for not rushing out, alone and unarmed, into the muzzles of all those blazing guns when there was no way that she could have saved her precious child. She would have been just one more body rotting under the tropical sun instead of becoming, as she did, the sole eyewitness to these hideous crimes that Salvadoran and U.S. officials denied repeatedly, elaborately, and falsely.[xii]

* * *

Galileo recanted what he knew to be factually true—that the Earth orbits the Sun—in order to assuage the prelates of his day who insisted that this fact contradicted the sense of the Scriptures. Shall we, unlike Peter, Antonio, Rufina, and Galileo, choose futile purity over preserving our opportunities to do actual good in the often-grim reality of God's world?

---

xii In *The Massacre at El Mozote* (Vintage Books, 1994), Mark Danner gives a full account of the massacre, the Salvadoran and U.S. cover-up efforts, Rufina Amaya's survival, and the guerrillas' revenge.

Christianity

Being a Christian seems to mean (a) believing in Jesus, which can mean many things; (b) trying to live by his teachings and example; and (c) for many Christians, accepting certain narratives and doctrines and participating in certain sacraments and rituals.

* * *

At the heart of being a good Christian, I believe, is the way we treat others. If it's with love and respect, we become our humble, gentle, loving best selves that I believe God and the Christianity of Jesus ask us to be.

* * *

What does it mean to "believe in God"? To believe certain propositions about God's attributes and accomplishments? Or that we should treat others as we believe God wishes? Or both? And what does it mean to "believe in Jesus"? To believe a specific narrative about his life, doings, words, death, resurrection, and kinship or oneness with God? Or that his teachings and example should guide us in the ways that God would have us live and treat others? Or both? Which do we suppose matters more to God and humankind and ourselves?

* * *

If I believe the authorized story about Jesus but don't help people in need, am I a Christian? If I help strangers in need but don't believe or even know the story, am I a Christian?

* * *

"If you don't believe in Jesus's resurrection, you can't be a Christian." How coercive! How untrue!

* * *

Some hazards and pitfalls: * Occupying oneself with one's beliefs about God and Jesus to the point of diverting oneself from what one does (or not) about other people. * Assuming that talking the talk without walking the walk suffices. * Focusing on getting into Heaven, getting the theology right, or mastering the Scriptures, all the while ignoring the needs of others.

* * *

According to a poll released in July 2013: "Nearly six out of ten Americans (59 percent) say that being a religious person 'is primarily about living a good life and doing the right thing,' as opposed to more than one third (36 percent) who hold that being religious is primarily about having faith and the right beliefs.'"[34]

It feels good to be in the majority now and then.

* * *

A friend who is a Catholic nun said she was sorry that the Christianity of Jesus—of peace, love, compassion, forgiveness, and the equality of "the least of these"[35] to everyone else—seems to have been taken over by the Christianity of Constantine, which finds greed, violence, imperialism, and war acceptable. Possibly the former Christianity has more adherents; but adherents of the latter seem to run our country and shape our history.

* * *

I asked an old friend who was a Protestant minister what effect he thought Constantine had on Christianity. His answer: "He ruined it."

* * *

After Constantine, Christianity too often served as a whore of empire, much as certain other religions served other empires, and provided faux justifications for fighting "just wars" and "projecting power," i.e., killing inconvenient people. Not what Jesus had in mind, I suppose. It's sobering that many Southerners are still said to believe that the cause of the Confederacy was godly and mainly about exercising freedom and state's rights, not about preserving slavery. Sure, it was about freedom and rights, killing hundreds of thousands of Americans to perpetuate the freedom and "right" to keep on stealing the labor and lives of millions of their fellow human beings and inculcating the racism that, in one way or another, plagues all Americans today.

* * *

Would the last two millennia of Western endeavors have been even bloodier if Jesus had not lived? Or, when one considers all the mischief done in Jesus's name, perhaps less bloody? Or did he have little or no effect on the depth of the ocean of blood?

* * *

Father Emmett A. Coyne warned in March 2015 that, "Christianity, if it remains aligned with nationalism, corporatism and social inequality, will bleed adherents."[36]

As it should.

* * *

U.S. society, we hear, is largely Christian and classless, yet a great many Americans reject the values of the itinerant Prince of Peace, who lived in poverty and befriended his society's outcasts. Jesus condemned hypocrites, yet hypocrisy about faith is more or less integral to many people's adjustment to life. La Rochefoucauld: "Hypocrisy is the homage that vice pays to virtue."

* * *

When a beggar comes through a subway car in New York City, it is most often, in my observation, the humbly dressed passengers who drop money into his or her cup while the expensively dressed people bury themselves in their *New York Times* or *Wall Street Journal.*

* * *

The Reverend Lee Moore, who worked with the Sunday school in which I once taught, used to say that Christianity is only one generation away from becoming extinct—that unless each new generation learns it, it's gone. A recent example is the reported racism and indifference of many U.S. troops to the lives and dignity of Iraqi civilians during the ill-conceived U.S. war in their homeland that began in 2003—"We sure lit up them ragheads!"—suggesting that many ostensibly civilized people live at the edge of the jungle and, on occasion, cross into it. While any religion may be one generation from extinction, the primitive ancestors within each of us face no such peril.

* * *

Commonly asked: "If we have sound ethics, why do we need religion?" Compassionate conduct may, of course, flow from either one. But while many people take comfort in the peace of God, who takes comfort in the peace of ethics? God inspires many, but whom does ethics inspire? And who thanks ethics for the blessings of this life?

* * *

Stuff about Jesus that we cannot verify—the circumstances of his birth, the reported miracles, his relationship with God, his resurrection, and so on— commands much attention from many Christians. But it's the verifiable stuff that he taught—for instance, that love, peace, forgiveness, and charity are best for us and others—that merits Christians' main focus.

* * *

Doctrine always means division, it often means diversion, and theological logic readily passes the point of being helpful.

* * *

The race may be to the swift and the prize to the strong, but peace is to the gentle.

* * *

Christianity may have remained as popular as it has over the centuries through the resonance between the life and words of Jesus and the godly element in so many people—more, one hopes, in spite of, not because of, the hype in some Scriptures and coercion by some clerics.

* * *

Christianity has often been made intimidating: Believe and you are saved; don't believe and you are damned or at least excluded. If you fear that believe-or-burn is the choice, then your response is easy. But do you truly believe what you're coerced or terrified into believing, or do you merely pay it lip service even in your heart? Coercion cheats Christianity and Christians. How can a faith induced by fear satisfy either God or people who strive to be faithful?

* * *

Many of us were brought up to believe that God tortures sinners forever in Hell. That strikes me as a gross slander of God that some Christian clerics have perpetuated for centuries in order to recruit, terrify, and control the faithful and even to make them godly.

* * *

To some extent, the spread of Christianity has depended on the creation of guilt feelings that we do not deserve and that I doubt that Jesus sought to instill. One hopes that the greater force has been the good news of the Gospels—even the parts I doubt, since I recognize that many of my doubts may be misplaced and I'm not sure which ones.

* * *

The Apostles' Creed and Nicene Creed, which I was brought up on, include elements that I find improbable (e.g., the resurrection of the body) and irrelevant to the godly ways to live and treat others. Yet people are admonished to accept these Creeds in toto, essentially on faith that the men who wrote them related the true facts about God, Jesus, the Holy Spirit, and so on, and that our believing all this pleases God.

* * *

Creeds are inherently confining. They limit our freedom to think for our-

selves and instead encourage, or demand, unquestioning acceptance. Indeed, that is part of their purpose. Presenting as they do an all-or-nothing
choice, they coerce those who would be faithful. I used to find it awkward
to join in reading aloud a creed or prayer during a church service, saying to
myself yes to this, maybe to that, and no to something else. When I find myself sitting in a service that includes such readings today, I usually remain
silent.

* * *

For Quakers, it's hard to have heresy since we don't have a formal creed. Yet
Quakers, too, feel pressures to conform.

* * *

Simplicity is a Quaker principle ("testimony"), plus it describes the Quaker
Way, a way that is also, in the words of British educator Ben Pink Dandelion, "not a place that claims to have all the answers but one which rather
encourages questions. It is a spiritual home which emphasizes seeking and
which is cautious about finally finding."[37] In my view, simplicity should be a
principle of Christianity in general—at least of the parts that matter. Why
would God or Jesus want it otherwise?

* * *

We don't need "intelligent design" in the classroom; we do need science in
the church and Sunday school, so that students learn there the realities of
God's marvelous creation.

* * *

If Jesus were always God, why did the Spirit descend upon him when he
encountered John the Baptist after he had grown to manhood? Why did he
err in his science, saying for instance that the world was about to end when
it wasn't? The claim of Athanasius of Alexandria that people could be saved
only if they accepted the view that Jesus was always God may have scared
many folks into agreeing; but from this distance, the claim looks like a coercive fiction that neither honors Jesus nor advances true Christianity.

* * *

Inspired as I believe Jesus was by some form of the Holy Spirit, he was not
devoid of human limits. It may be natural for many Christians to stress or
inflate his virtues and minimize or deny his limits, but I think that in the
long run—which may now have arrived—it serves both Jesus and Christianity if we see him, as best we can, as he was.

* * *

Is capitalism compatible with Christianity? To the extent that *capitalism* means that the race for riches is to the swift, the Devil takes the hindmost, and to hell with prudent regulations and a safety net for impoverished people, then it does not sound Christian to me. And it gives a bad name to the capitalists who respect their workers and customers, deal fairly with them, and don't dodge the taxes that pay for the government services that they rely on.

* * *

Quakerism began as a purely Christian denomination. Our founder, George Fox, had an epiphany in 1647 when, as a young seeker fasting and wandering through Derbyshire in the English Midlands, he said he perceived a voice saying, "'There is one, even Christ Jesus, that can speak to thy condition,' and when I heard it my heart did leap for joy."[38] Shortly thereafter, Fox began making converts, thus launching the Religious Society of Friends, commonly called Quakers. Today many of us remain wholly committed Christians while many others are more or less universalists in that we draw more heavily on other sources and less, if at all, on Jesus. There is no bright line dividing the two groups; rather, we stand along a spectrum.

At least two reasons appear for the rise of universalist Quakers: One is an influx of "Quakers by convincement" (i.e., by conversion, as opposed to being "birthright Quakers") who began their spiritual journeys as Protestants, Catholics, Jews, agnostics, or other non-Christians. Second and I think more significant is the Quaker view that since everyone has a godly element and may receive divine guidance, we do well to recognize revelations, as best we can, from many sources and traditions, not solely Jesus or the Bible.

* * *

So where do I stand on the spectrum? I suppose that if ten is wholly Christian and one is wholly universalist, I am at six or seven. Nancy supposes that she is too.

* * *

For most Christians, a priest, minister, or other clergy serves as an intermediary between God and themselves, while Quakers who belong to "unprogrammed," that is, silent Meetings, seek a direct relationship with God. While we of the latter tradition may gain in freedom and responsibility, we miss the learning, perspective, and perhaps orthodoxy of a professional cleric. We are encouraged to make up the difference by reading, study, reflection, and conversation.

* * *

While Quakers do not have a formal creed and I cannot speak for other Quakers—though you may have noticed that I talk about them—it's my observation that Quakers generally base our actions less on specific Scriptures than on our "testimonies" (values) of peace, equality, integrity, simplicity, community, stewardship, and service. But these testimonies are, in good part, distillations of the teachings of Jesus and, not coincidentally, of other great prophets.

* * *

St. Benedict and Quakers: "Listen with the ear of our heart and hear the voice of God"—though it's often hard to differentiate one's heart from one's ego, self-interest, hormonal promptings, and so on. Many people listen to their guts, which speak soundly sometimes. This heart and gut reside, of course, not in our torso but in our mind.

* * *

At the start of a Meeting for Worship, we Quakers ideally "center down" by clearing our minds and "wait upon the word of the Lord," which may come, if at all, as a "still, small voice," which ordinary thoughts would have drowned out if we had not cleared them away. Isn't that essentially the same as Benedict's listening with the ear of one's heart to hear the voice of God? And one needn't be a Catholic or a Quaker to do it.

* * *

Reading the preeminent book of Taoism, the *Tao Te Ching*, I have been struck by the Friendliness of the Christian values that it preaches: the meek shall inherit the earth; the first shall be last; don't contend with those who wrong you but turn the other cheek; only by losing your life shall you save it; the wages of sin are a kind of living death. Plus simplicity, humility, the evil and futility of war, the virtue of not getting worked up over material things, and so on.

* * *

Two great religions, Christianity and Taoism, teach us in effect to restrain some of our God-given natural instincts. Were Jesus and Lao Tzu among God's agents for accelerating our moral evolution?

* * *

It helps for Christians to see other faiths—Judaism, Buddhism, Hinduism, Taoism, Islam, et al.—not as erring or competing, but rather as affirming Christianity to the extent that they all share similar insights and, in particular, value compassion, as they all seem to. If there is an echo of God in everyone, it follows that the soundest parts of the main religions resemble each other, as they seem to. Religions resemble each other most in the aspects that matter the most—not the ancient narratives but the way we treat folks. I suppose God wants it this way.

* * *

We can focus on how similar Christianity is to other religions or how different. What do we gain by doing the latter? Concluding that we have the best may help our ego but what else?

* * *

"We [Christians] recognize ourselves in the true image of other believers, in the Qur'an or in the Torah. We believers encourage each other over the barriers raised by people who do not wish any of us well."

— Garry Wills[39]

* * *

I used to think that an ecumenical Christianity that had everyone attending the same church would be ideal, until I saw that people of differing temperaments worship best in different ways. Some are most at home with structure and ritual; some are not. Some seek a direct relationship with God; most prefer an ordained intermediary. Some can sit for an hour in silence; most can't—at least not comfortably. So let there be diversity and harmony among churches.

* * *

If Christianity were naïve, foolish, or wrong, then why are so many who try to practice it such decent people? The same may be asked about non-violent Buddhists, Jews, Muslims, and members of other serious faiths, which after all, make common appeals to our higher natures.

* * *

Nationalism and particularly U.S. exceptionalism strike me as ungodly and unchristian insofar as they encourage Americans to suppose that our own lives have greater value than the lives of other peoples, or that what is wrong for others to do is O.K for us. U.S. exceptionalism denies the fellowship of humankind. The 3,000 Americans killed in the 9/11 terrorist attack helped to "justify" the needless killing of hundreds of thousands of Iraqi civilians and uncounted thousands of Afghan civilians in our wars of choice, that is, in our homicidal lashing out at millions of innocent people. The official U.S. refusal to count the Iraqi civilians whom we killed told the world that for us those Iraqi lives did not count. Constantine trumped Jesus again, and no doubt more foreigners than ever learned to love America instead of joining terrorist groups.

* * *

I love my country enough to find claims of "American exceptionalism" embarrassing.

* * *

There are no foreigners, at least not for followers of Jesus and other cosmopolitan prophets.

* * *

A thinking Christian is likely agnostic about much. We are told much that is actually unknowable. Accept it on faith? Why?

* * *

From the Quaker belief that all people may speak from their own godly Inward Light, it follows that neither Jesus nor anyone else has delivered the last word of divine revelation. The letters of Paul and the messages of Buddha, Lao Tzu, Mohammed, philosophers, poets, writers, preachers, and others—not to mention the sciences—constantly complement, refine, amplify, and add to it. It's a challenge to recognize actual revelations as and when they surface. Revelations will expand and refresh us as long as people seek and reflect and listen to their own still, small voice.

* * *

Many Quakers and, I understand, people of other Christianities report that they have felt unity with God or Jesus or both. Not me. The nearest I come to such spiritual ecstasy is when I feel very close to other people or the great outdoors.

* * *

Rereading these pages tells me that I have more negative feelings than I had realized about the Christianity of Constantine and today's believers who don't have a problem with materialism, American exceptionalism, and even militarism. But the Christianity of Jesus is wonderful and so, for the most part, are the people who take it to heart—whether or not I agree with their versions of it.

Faith

They take you at a gullible age, tell you an improbable tale, and assure you that the loving God will roast you in Hell forever if you don't believe the whole megillah. Fear makes a fragile foundation for faith.

* * *

Since God chose to be mysterious, why should we not be curious? Surely skepticism is not evil, nor can it be it a sin to question an improbable tale. Doubting Thomas had the makings of an able lawyer or realistic theologian. Blind faith may be for many but not for me.

* * *

I suppose that most people start out being told about religion at home, in Sunday school, and in church. One's spiritual development and appreciation of God gain depth—some may say, lose depth—when one starts questioning what one is told. At least mine did.

* * *

Faith is said to heal on Earth and lead to Heaven. Jesus told a number of people that their faith had healed their afflictions, implying, I suppose, that if one isn't healed, one's faith must be wanting. And Jesus encouraged strong and unquestioning faith more directly, too. But many pretenders have encouraged the same. I do not see virtue in following a prophet like incurious sheep, nor vice in questioning, probing, and trying to figure it all out. Like here.

* * *

A religious education may be necessary in forming one's faith and, after a point that varies from person to person, an obstacle to developing it.

* * *

Perhaps the ultimate act of faith is to treat others as we would have them treat us. But regardless of one's faith or lack thereof, it's the kind thing to do.

* * *

To the extent that faith is not based on knowledge, it is inherently precarious and subject to falling short or reaching too far. I find it easy to believe in

God and impossible to believe in a Trinity. But many good people do believe in the Trinity, and I cannot assure you that I am right and they are not.

* * *

I cannot believe that what we believe, which for most of us is what other people taught us to believe, matters more than what we do. Yet my beliefs inform my actions, and my actions that accord with my faith tend to be better for everyone they touch than my actions that do not. I suppose the same is true for most people of faith.

* * *

Many spiritual people aren't simply *believers* or *agnostics*. Rather, we believe some things, disbelieve some, and doubt or have no opinion about the rest. After we reach a certain age, some people, especially men—especially me?—need an infusion of humility to save themselves from expressing opinions about everything.

* * *

The array of facts, words, and events that we are told about God, Jesus, and so on strikes me as ranging from almost surely true to most unlikely. It follows that it's unreasonable and unfair to expect, much less demand, that a person believe the whole of any package. At the same time, it's unsound to disbelieve it all simply because some of it defies belief. Happily, the least credible assertions tend to be the least significant. "Love thy neighbor" is essential, but reports that Jesus "walked on water" or "raised the dead" don't affect to the way I live.

* * *

Physicist Werner Heisenberg espoused the uncertainty principle for quantum mechanics in the 1920s; and I am among those who espouse an uncertainty principle for theology, that is, I cannot answer many of the great questions with any certainty. Inconsequential agnosticisms lie scattered harmlessly across my faith. It's tragic that so many people have fought and died over one illusory certainty or another.

* * *

Paradoxically, some propositions of faiths seem to gain credibility from seeming unbelievable. "Jesus arose from the dead." Quakers largely avoid the issue by having no creed, though we are still expected to believe that there's That of God in everyone, all are equal before God, and so on. *Trust in God* comes easily to me without a need for sorting out elements of faith—trust, not that God necessarily protects me, certainly not that God manages the details of my life, but that God abides with me as I let God, through the ups and downs of the life that God has given me. *Thy will, however inscrutable, be done.*

* * *

I feel that I have led an incredibly fortunate life. Did God arrange it this way, or was I lucky?

* * *

Faith becomes destructive when people try to impose their version of it, and the conduct they think it requires, upon others. It is one thing to offer your beliefs to others (as this book sort of does), quite another to try to coerce them on the basis of what you believe and they don't yet. That's a power trip that they don't need and we do well not to indulge in.

* * *

What was the point of having colonies unless the imperialists could steal the resources, labor, and often the lives of the locals and impose their faith upon the survivors? For decades the U.S. (though not actually having colonies except the islands we call "territories") has sought to impose its faith in a highly flawed capitalism and democracy as broadly as possible. President Nixon reportedly caused the U.S. to support the violent overthrow of the elected government of Chile in1973 because he feared that its socialism would *succeed* and thereby set a "bad example" for the Hemisphere.

* * *

A challenge to faith is to separate reality from fantasy. How, if at all, does our faith affect us and the people whose lives we touch? A test of faith is whether and how it stands up to life's realities. In the 1960s, for instance, the astute duo Simon and Garfunkel, in their hit song about a movie character named Mrs. Robinson, sang that Jesus loves this conniving adulteress more than she will know. When I asked my junior high Sunday school students whether Jesus would love a person like her, most of them agreed that he would. Mrs. Robinson was fictional; but if the Christian message is sound, so were the students who agreed.

* * *

Our friend Delores says that her spirituality consists of being sufficiently awake to catch the God that is happening around her and in her.

* * *

The faith of many people in their God seems to thrive despite the awful things such as the Holocaust, famines, wars, and cruel diseases that befall strangers. But let something awful happens to us personally or to someone we love, and our faith may vanish amid a storm of bitterness and feelings that we've been betrayed. Or, our acceptance of God may grow more consistent with God's world as it is. Or, first the one and then the other—like going through stages of grief.

* * *

Many people seem to believe that God micromanages everyone's life, decides what good or bad things will happen to each of us, and makes our decisions for us—moreover, that God does all this for billions of people more ably than a grand master may play a mere twenty games of chess against twenty opponents at the same time—so that we are but puppets who delude ourselves that we're free. Then when harm befalls such believers or their loved ones, they may blame God or reject God. Or reality may deepen their faith as they realize that God is not as they had thought or been taught. While it is hard to say what God is, it may be painful to say that God is not the ever-saving lifeguard on life's beach.

* * *

Remaining faithful to God through terrible times helps to sustain us through those times. That is a gift that God gives us if we give it to ourselves. Like many gifts from God, all we need to do to receive it is to open ourselves to accepting it.

* * *

If we love God the Creator, then we love the God that created tigers, typhoons, cockroaches, rats, and the tapeworms that may live in the guts of a starving child. We may (or may not) believe that God, in God's own way, loves us and may also love those hurtful vermin in all their richness and destructiveness.

* * *

Fiercely held myths of the past need not constrain us, but they often do. Pilate asked, What is truth? (John 18:38) Likewise: What is myth? And what myths are true?

* * *

Paradoxically perhaps, our spiritual journey is a journey towards reality.

* * *

Scholarship that shows the errors and inconsistencies in our surviving copies of the Scriptures have, theoretically at least, given people of faith new leave to question passages that seem incongruous or wrong or even right.

* * *

Being faithful to Jesus requires us to be unfaithful to some passages of the Gospels that many people call the immutable Word of God. Rejecting such passages is easier to do than it used to be, now that scholarship has shown the extent to which the Scriptures that have reached us are not, or may not be, accurate copies of lost originals. Does this put scholarship above the Word of God? No, it puts it above the fallible scribes, copiers, and translators through whom we receive what men once wrote down as the Word of God.

* * *

Many things seem to work out better for those who love the Lord and their fellow human beings. Is this a manifestation of the power of love? Or of God, or of both? Or wishful thinking?

* * *

Faith can be a lose-lose proposition: If we don't have it, we miss a lot; if we do have it, prior theologians may have loaded our version of it with so much baggage—damnation, Hell, Original Sin, and so on—that it's almost sure to keep us anxious. Unless we run the risk of dumping the baggage that doesn't ring true. The Gospel is supposed to be Good News, not Bad News.

* * *

Many people respond to life's ambiguities by cloaking themselves in illusions of certainty. Unless we are content to believe what we've been taught, we do well to examine our preconceptions and received wisdom in order to recognize and explore the ambiguities that comprise so much of reality, that is, to run the risks of being seekers.

* * *

When Evangelicals perceive that they hear God speaking to them, they tend, logically and conscientiously, to believe and obey. In contrast, when Quakers think we've found some insight from our Inward Light, many of us question and test it rather than accept it uncritically.

* * *

It's fine with me that many people are certain that various articles of their faith are sound. I do find it refreshing, though, that Quakers tend to believe a few things deeply and to act on their beliefs. I suppose that one test of a faith is the extent to which its adherents feel free to question its tenets. Some faiths tolerate or even encourage seekers; some discourage or even expel them; but it's a mistake for us who follow the former to see no merit in the latter.

* * *

Quakers tend to test what we're told by seeing if it resonates with our better angels (That of God within us). The similarities in the resonances among all peoples may help to account for the fact that the religions of the world that became widely popular have fundamental similarities. The great faiths tend to converge on the great truths that echo within all peoples.

* * *

Faith implies uncertainty—except for those who feel certain in their faith. For the rest of us, the challenge is to live faithfully in spite of the uncertainties and, if we care to, try to demark the line between faith and illusion.

* * *

We can be wholly certain, or we can question and glimpse parts of the truth part of the time. Which way yields more truth? I don't know. Which stimulates more thought? That's easy.

* * *

Certainty, however comfortable, quashes the quest for truth. But can faith live without certainty? Mine does—not about God the Creator, but about much else.

* * *

For me, loving God is more an idea than an emotion.

* * *

Fairly late in life I learned that some people whose faithfulness I admire seek in this life to come into the presence of God or be united with God. Having learned it, I have not sought it, except to listen for the still, small voice within me. This life and world and people are more than enough for me for now.

* * *

It sounds wonderful when people say they experience God, have a personal relationship with God, or feel unity with God; but I do not. I feel endless admiration for God and gratitude to God; I try to act in accord with what I believe God wants; but I have not felt myself to be in touch with the Great Mystery. That's okay with me, and I hope it is with God.

* * *

The mighty furnace of the Sun burns on for eons while the rocky planets toast almost like marshmallows on very long sticks as they orbit through a void that's nearly as cold as cold can be. Mercury and Venus are too hot for life as we know it, Mars is too hostile, and Earth remains remarkably right (though ignorant, greedy, and many wealthy people seem bent on ending that). A red and green hummingbird appears to hang motionless as it hovers an inch from Nancy's red plastic feeder in a breeze that is gusting fitfully to twenty knots. Do we take such marvels for granted? What is faith without a sense of wonder?

* * *

The Scriptures put great store in believing in God. Abraham's willingness to sacrifice Isaac, Job's perseverance in spite of the calamities that befell him, give prominent examples of men whose faith survived extreme tests. The Gospel of John teaches that "God so loved the world that he gave his only Son, that everyone who believes in him may not perish but may have eternal life." (John 3:16) According to Christian traditions, if you separate yourself from God, the consequences are dire. But now that many people pay little attention to these examples, traditions, and threats, they may finally be able to decide for themselves, without fear or coercion, *of their own free will,* whether or not to believe in God and heed God's still, small voice within themselves, not to mention all the instructions that come at them from the Bible and other sources. This strikes me as progress. I hope God thinks so too.

Miracles

I wrote this. You are reading it. Two miracles right here.

* * *

On October 25, 2012, a jet plane flew Nancy and me from Boston to Chicago. If that weren't miracle enough, that evening Pat Barker's *The Eye in the Door* took me to the England of a century ago.

* * *

Jesus's first miracle was said to be turning water into wine, and who believes it? Yet people constantly turn wine into urine, and who considers that a miracle? Besides me.

* * *

There are two kinds of miracles: The first are those, which the term commonly calls to mind, that seem to contravene nature; but either they accord with an aspect of nature that's beyond our ken or they probably did not happen. Second are those that are unquestionably real, that we often take for granted, and that come from Creation in all its glory. How miraculous it is that the relatively benign Earth has swung through the frigid violence of the void as it has for several billion years.

* * *

"There are only two ways to live your life. One is as though nothing is a miracle. The other is as though everything is a miracle."

—Albert Einstein[40]

* * *

On most dry days when the temperature was between 20 and 80 degrees during nearly thirty years, I walked part way down and up the mountain road that Nancy and I lived on—a miracle and a blessing. How many miracles we take for granted! And how many blessings!

* * *

"Our human bodies are miracles, not because they defy laws of nature, but precisely because they obey them."

—Rabbi Harold S. Kushner[41]

* * *

Consider the miracle of the Sun. When I built a fire in my high-tech wood-stove and set the air vent properly, the logs gave off heat for several hours before they turned to embers and either I put on more logs or the room began to cool. In contrast, the nuclear fire in our Sun, which I'm told is a very ordinary star, has been scattering its energy in every direction for the past several billion years with such ferocity that the minuscule portion that reaches the ping pong ball called Earth ninety-three million miles across the frigid void is sufficient to sustain life and prompt millions of well-off people to air-condition their homes. While no one has been throwing fresh logs on the Sun, we are told that it will burn as fiercely for another several billion years and not go out like an ordinary fire but still have enough energy to end in a grand explosion.

* * *

The energy that has burned long enough and fiercely enough to permit us to evolve is same energy that may well enable us, absent nuclear disarmament, to end life on Earth.

* * *

Consider, too, the sub miracle of photosynthesis: radiance from this star empowers plants to make most of the oxygen and food that sustain the lives of us and the other animals including the animals we eat.

* * *

It's no surprise that so many people believe in God when the choice is God (or gods) or nothing. But the custom of many millions of people to leave their homes every week on a morning when they don't have to and sit for an hour or so in a long room and worship, pay homage to, sing about, and sometimes think about God is remarkable—perhaps even a miracle.

* * *

If science explains an apparent miracle, does that destroy its miraculousness? If one defines a miracle as an event that defies the laws of Nature, and science then shows that the event actually accords with those laws, then the answer is yes—even though the event is exactly what it was before it was explained. But for me, a miracle is something absolutely wonderful; and the world is full of them, so full that most of us take most of them for granted most of the time with nary a thought about how truly miraculous they are. Indeed, the laws of Nature are themselves miraculous, and I believe they govern everything that happens. It's not that an event beyond our ken is unnatural; it's that our ignorance may make it seem so. Yet I can't deny that events that violate natural laws may happen or that Jesus may have performed some.

* * *

It is our understanding of how God operates through the laws of Nature that makes it hard to believe some of the miracles reported in the Gospels. We say that God can do anything, but many of us have trouble accepting that God may, at Jesus's instance, have suspended or defied the natural laws that God created. Yet even today it is common to hear of "miraculous" escapes from death and recoveries from illness, especially when people have been praying for the person who is sick or in peril. I expect we hear less about it when the prayers don't work.

* * *

Miracles reported in the Scriptures: My faith does not depend on alleged violations or suspensions of natural laws.

* * *

Presumably the God that had the power to create the laws of Nature has the power to suspend them, but why would God do that? Why would God, through Jesus or anyone else, raise a few people from the dead for a few years but later allow Hitler to murder ten million people?

* * *

Analyzing the likelihood that Jesus actually performed the various miracles attributed to him does not strike me as a useful exercise, even if one decides that he performed at least some of them. If the words and example of Jesus reflect God's way, what do the miracles that he did or did not perform matter to us today? And if his lessons do not reflect God's way, what does it matter what miracles he performed? The report that Jesus revived the corpse of Lazarus has no bearing on the soundness of loving thy neighbor.

* * *

During Jesus's time, the reports of his miracles and the extent to which he fulfilled various earlier prophecies probably cloaked him with the Divine authority and thus helped to convince many people that he taught God's ways, thereby getting Christianity accepted and its message taken seriously. Today, the same stories, being widely disbelieved, tend to be irrelevant or, worse, to undermine Jesus's credibility about God's ways. What matters now is the truth and resonance of his message, while many of us disbelieve the implausible stuff or relegate it to the realm of symbolism or mystery or irrelevancy.

* * *

Let's face it, some reported miracles may have been hype to sell the faith.

* * *

We are told to take the improbable parts of the Gospels as symbols or allegories or errors in transcription or translation; but were at least some of them simply fabrications calculated to sell Christianity, false advertising in a holy cause?

* * *

Who has not wondered which Biblical miracles, if any, were actually tall tales designed to sell the faith?

* * *

I can believe the Gospel accounts of some miracles, if that matters, but not all of them. I doubt, for instance, that Jesus walked on water or revived a corpse that was truly decomposing or turned water into wine. Such accounts seem not only implausible but also irrelevant to the truth of his message. I have no doubt, though, about the miracles of a Sun that is neither too young nor old and an Earth that is neither too warm nor cold. Likewise for the miracles of water, fire, love, music, cooking, sex, beauty, the atom, evolution, gravity, language, memory, and the nurturing gases that envelop the Earth. And life after death? No more unlikely than life after birth.

* * *

To recapitulate the many miracles that comprise the miracle of Creation: Scientists tell us that near the beginning of the present era of Creation, roughly 13.8 billion years ago—that is, near the Big Bang or whatever it was that started this cosmos—the totality of the commonly known elements consisted of hydrogen, which comprised about three quarters of all non-dark matter, and helium, which comprised nearly all the rest. Gravity drew clouds of these elements together into masses that, as they grew bigger, formed themselves into spheres and ignited into the thermonuclear fireballs that we call stars. The furnaces of these stars, and the explosions that finally blew them apart, forged their hydrogen and helium into the heavier elements and propelled them off into space like shrapnel from a bursting bomb. The bigger the stars, the faster they burned out—perhaps within a few million years—and the heavier the elements they created. Gradually again, some of these heavy elements—oxygen, carbon, iron, lead, and the rest—coalesced into masses which, as they grew, became the spheres we call planets. The masses that remained relatively small are called comets and asteroids and meteors and exist in any old shape. The mass of Earth may seem large to us, but the Sun is more than 300,000 times larger. The gravity of many stars held many planets nearby, yet the speed of the planets' forward motion through space created the centrifugal force that kept them orbiting their stars instead of falling into them and burning up.

Consider the miracle of this process by which clouds of light gases developed over billions of years into us. Every rock and pebble, every drop of water in every wave and every beach it breaks upon, and every particle of our bodies comes from stuff that those exploding stars blasted into space billions of years gone by. Ashes to ashes, and stardust to stardust.

How did hydrogen and helium, the original building blocks of the heavier elements, come into being? If we say the Big Bang did it, presumably that only points to a step in a process and raises the further questions of what caused the Big Bang and what enabled it to proceed as it did? What gave these light elements a nature that would cause or allow intense heat and pressure to bulk up their atoms into totally different elements? Who would have thought that planets can and commonly do go into orbit around stars and remain in that improbable balance of forces for billions of years? How does it happen that there are a gravity and a centrifugal force that have the power to perform their crucial tasks?

Consider the atmosphere that lets the rays of the Sun that make life possible pass through it, yet protects us (now less than before) from their death-dealing power. Or consider the more basic miracle that matter is an inert form of energy and energy is a dynamic form of matter, in a ratio that Einstein famously expressed as e = mc2. Less dramatically, the miracle that ice is a form of water, and water is a form of ice and so is steam.

The fact that science may describe the laws of physics and probability that permit these miracles to occur does not diminish their miraculousness. Rather, it illuminates it.

Consider, too, the infinitesimal atom. Ask how electrons, protons, and neutrons acquired the properties that allowed or compelled them to form the atoms that comprise every thing we know about, how adding or subtracting protons, neutrons, or electrons causes them to change their properties radically and gain or lose the ability to combine into still different molecules. Burn (oxidize) hydrogen and you get water. How did it come to pass that electrons were able to join protons one way to form neutrons and another way to form atoms? Answers to these questions will do nothing to diminish their miraculousness.

Some scientists inclined to atheism say that, given the ability of DNA to instruct the offspring of any being on how to construct itself into a new and largely identical being, plus the incidence of mutations, plus the length of time that Earth has had a temperate climate and plentiful water, plus the relative rarity of devastating asteroid strikes, then it follows that the earliest one-cell bits of life have had the *time* and *capacity* to evolve into higher life forms like us all without Divine assistance. Note that these scientists have not proved and cannot prove that this *did happen*, but only, they say, that it *could have* happened without God—given, somehow, the properties of the building blocks and applicable forces whose creation their atheism does *not* explain. More to the point, each of the givens in their sequence did not have to be.

While Chance may well have played a role in all this (which star captured which planet and so forth), the extent to which the whole process has succeeded in producing and sustaining life as we know it strikes me as being a stupendous and most unlikely miracle—most unlikely, that is, without the hand of God.

* * *

Even as science has opened our eyes to many miracles of the natural world, it has tended to close our eyes to the extrasensory perceptions that so many people feel they have experienced.

* * *

The overarching miracle is that you and I and the universe exist. For nothing to exist would have been so much simpler, but here we are.

* * *

The clear lesson of the miracle stories in the Gospels is that Jesus often tried to help strangers in need.

People

We are endowed with spirit, mind, and flesh. May we give thanks for and delight in each.

* * *

So far as I know, we humans stand at a pinnacle of God's creation—the most creative, accomplished, and destructive of God's creatures on Earth. We owe God thanks and praise for all people, albeit more for most than for some; yet limits on population are dangerously overdue.

* * *

Consider the vast sacrilege of war, the willful smashing of God's living temples.

* * *

Some say we are a little below the angels. How presumptuous! We are a little above the ants.

* * *

It is said that the human heart is the true temple of God. Isn't it also the lair of Satan?

* * *

When the authors of Genesis wrote that God created man in God's image, they apparently conceived of God as an elderly superman roaming close by in their small corner of the Middle East. The more we know about the vastness and complexity of Creation, the more outlandish it is to suppose that we humans, with our many faults, exist in the image of the Great Mystery who created it all.

* * *

The Bible seems to assume that it's been all downhill since God banished well-evolved Adam and Eve from the Garden of Eden. In fact it's been an ascent since the first creatures emerged from the sea. The fall of Man? No, it's been the rise of humankind.

* * *

The General Confession in *The Book of Common Prayer*, which I had to memorize in my Episcopal Church confirmation class, says in part, "We have left undone those things which we ought to have done; And we have done those things which we ought not to have done; And there is no health in us." Yes. Yes. No! I did not then and do not now agree that there is no health in you and me. Such often insincere protestations of unworthiness belong to a Christian tradition that has dogged me throughout my journey. For instance, the monk Thomas Merton, whom many revere, taught that, "Our meditation should begin with the realization of our nothingness and helplessness in the presence of God."[42] No, it should not. (Are we not the hands of God on Earth, hands that often drop the ball?) One may understand such self-abasing before the Almighty; but indulging in it is inaccurate and debases the One who created us, as well as the person proclaiming it. For if we humans, who are one of God's highest creations, tell God that we are nothing, aren't we impugning some of God's best work? I would agree that before God we are hugely puny and flawed—would agree, that is, except that I think it's presumptuous and pointless to compare ourselves to God in any way at all. There is a significant difference between being nothing and almost nothing. Ask the busy ant, who is less than us yet also marvelous.

* * *

If we are in God's image and there is no health in us, is there any health in God?

* * *

To the extent that being in God's image implies the converse—that God is in the image of us puny mammals—it demeans God to a point of a foolishness that verges on blasphemy.

* * *

Thy unworthy servant? No. Thy flawed but reasonably worthy servant as servants go.

* * *

In the present age of scientific revelation, it is even more pretentious to claim that on this one of a zillion planets in this one of a zillion galaxies whirling across time and the heavens, we, though fairly advanced among animals, are in the image of the God that made it all happen. Yet it seems, not presumptuous, but plausible to suppose that God evolved us, and perhaps other living beings across the cosmos, so that the still, small voice of God—audible to those who listen for it—resonates within the best part of each of us.

* * *

One point that we humans seem to have in common with God is that we exist, we live, we for a moment and God apparently forever, we of modest intellects and God of vast intelligence. The bit of God within us seems to include life itself.

* * *

All people, however virtuous, lovely, evil, or repulsive, share their humanity and the That of God within them, which is the best part of their humanity—however effectively some people ignore or suppress it.

* * *

All peoples that I know about have in common, in one form or another: families, music, stories, religion, war, and a minority who work for peace. At times, some of these traits negatively reinforce each other. Think of Richard Wagner's heroic music, of "Onward, Christian Soldiers," "The Battle Hymn of the Republic," and the martial marches of John Phillip Sousa, which I found perilously inspiring and empowering when I'd be walking over the ground in step with several hundred other soldiers. We were invincible, and anyone who challenged us would regret it. Yeah, right. The God of the Old Testament was, among other things, a war god, enabling Jews to survive and sometimes screw up. (Like today.) Today a number of religions oppose war; and if they and their unchurched allies should gain the upper hand, humankind has a chance.

* * *

The staff of New York City's Fortune Society, which assists convicts to return to society after they have served their time in prison, assures them that they are better than the worst thing they have ever done. How kind, useful, and contrary to the popular view of people who have committed even murder. I think the sentiment fits most people. Was Hitler better than World War Two or the Holocaust?

* * *

Interesting that so many people want to save the world. This is not always a blessing.

* * *

All labor that humans perform has dignity. It all deserves respect and fair wages.

* * *

"A lot of people don't want to be compassionate," said Karen Armstrong on NPR's "Fresh Air" on Monday, September 21, 2009. "They'd rather be right."

* * *

Only a few people achieve what is commonly called greatness, but everyone can be a decent person. What will today's greatness gain anyone in tomorrow's afterlife if there is one, or in the grave? But being a kind, gentle, and helpful soul gains us peace now and hopefully hereafter.

* * *

I have long thought it likely that Western civilization reached its pinnacle with the first performance of Beethoven's Ninth Symphony in Vienna on May 7, 1824, notwithstanding the progress since then in saving lives, taking lives, and making indoor plumbing widely available.

* * *

All people are temples of God? Consider the bloody bodies of previously healthy young men piled up at battles, the unarmed person most often a Black who is shot by a cop, the convict sometimes innocent whom the government executes.

* * *

A great many of my aged college classmates have written in our class update reports that—without mentioning the wealth or eminence they did or did not attain—they find their greatest pride and pleasure in their children and grandchildren. What does this suggest about God, ambition, family, and the best we can achieve in life?

* * *

If my spirituality centers on my relationship with God, then it includes my relationship with the whisper of God within you and every other person I encounter.

* * *

If we think that we humans have it tough, consider the other animals: Only adults in their prime or at the top of the food chain do not live in constant peril of becoming another animal's lunch. Here in Vermont, one may consider what it's like to be one of the creatures that live out in the weather the year round. They may survive in freezing rain or at thirty below, but they can't be all that comfortable. The dens where the bears hibernate may be sheltered but are not heated. Fortunately for the wildlife, the climate change ignorers and deniers and underachievers who control our government keep making our winters milder—which cannot compensate for the vast damage these people are enabling and doing to the whole planet.

* * *

It is so unjust that the people who have the power to control global warming but fail to control it have ready access to air-conditioning.

* * *

While I cannot swear that the deity called the Devil does not exist, I do not hold any exterior spirit responsible for my own harmful deeds. The Devil, if there is one, didn't make me do it. If there is a bit of God within us, is there also a bit of Evil? I think, rather, that we can and often do hurt others out of our own selfish or insensitive or playful desires and instincts. If compassion is the greatest virtue, then self-centeredness may be the seminal vice. If parents do not lead their children away from the self-centeredness they are necessarily born with, and towards the compassion that makes them fully human, then these parents are complicit in much of the harm that their children inflict on others and themselves as time goes by.

* * *

Free love: Sexual love can be most free when bound by commitment to another person. So often an affair becomes serious for one person while remaining casual for the other. Back when I was teaching junior high and high school kids in Sunday school, a football star named Joe Namath claimed to have copulated with 300 women during his years in college. I'd ask the class whether they would rather have sex once with 300 people they didn't know very well or 300 times with one person they loved. I expect you know their answer. Is it yours?

* * *

People need to love and be loved as much as they need to eat and sleep, though often not as evidently, and evidently not as often.

* * *

Paradox: In ancient times, a tribe apparently needed to be aggressive to survive. Today it requires the suppression or sublimation of that trait for the world to survive.

* * *

Jesus taught us to love our neighbors. That was probably necessary because there is a strong if often unspoken tendency to be wary of our neighbors, especially those who are "different," at least until they prove to be safe. Oscar Hammerstein II wrote in the lyrics for the 1949 hit show *South Pacific* that you've got to be carefully taught to hate and fear people who are different; but I am pretty certain that the opposite is true. Back in the day probably, people and tribes that were not leery of the "other" did not survive. But consider the instruction in the ancient Book of Leviticus 19:34 to love the stranger who dwells among you as yourself. Nowadays animosity towards those who are "different" causes much needless trouble, to put it mildly. A hashtag of the Friends Committee on National Legislation (a Quaker lobbying group) reads, "# Love Thy Neighbor (No Exceptions),"

* * *

Author Malcolm Braly wrote that sharing a cell with many different men during his years in several prisons taught him that one man is pretty much like another. Though I grew up in the so-called melding pot of Brooklyn, I didn't have much experience with Black people until I had several Black roommates and followed the orders of many Black corporals and sergeants in the army; and I saw that they were pretty much like everybody else.

* * *

While we may be as unique as our fingerprints, we are as similar as our hands—regardless of their hue.

* * *

God's economy: The woman grows the breasts that help to attract the man to participate in conceiving the baby whom the breasts will nourish.

* * *

"Whenever I meet a 'foreigner,' I always have the same feeling: 'I am meeting another member of the human family.'"
— His Holiness the Dalai Lama[43]

* * *

Like the Declaration of Independence but not the Constitution, Quakers stand for the equality of every person. Meaning what? Certainly not that all are equal in their physical, mental, or moral attributes; or the extent to which society's deck is stacked for or against them; or their accomplishments or luck good and bad. Yet one person's life is intrinsically worth no more or less than another's. The life of an American and an Iraqi, an Israeli and a Palestinian, a Brit and a Pakistani, a white and a black, a Christian and a Muslim, and so on, all have the same worth, the same brotherhood and sisterhood in the human family. So we are told, but how many people are sure it's true?

* * *

Equality, though basic, has its limits: Am I the equal of Jesus? No. Was Hitler the equal of me? No, though he was doubtless a more rousing speaker. The key, for Quakers at least, is that all of us have That of God within us, Jesus more than me, I more than Hitler or at least more evidently.

* * *

Just as we are all entitled to equal rights and the deference due to every human, we all bear a measure of responsibility to care for every creature great and small and the Earth on which we live and will die. But St. Francis I'm not. I killed the mice that got into the house where they destroyed stuff; then I admired their exquisite little feet. Nancy stuffed crumpled tinfoil into the cracks in the basement walls to keep them out in the cold, and she is skillful with the flyswatter.

* * *

Free will: Choosing can be hard. Ants, we are told, do not have to choose. But who would choose to be an ant?

* * *

Some people simply complain about problems. Others seek to solve them.

* * *

It is widely considered unmanly to weep. For me, weeping is self-help. Failing to feel free to weep, on the other hand, could stunt my compassion.

* * *

Apart from people's reflexive responses, sexual orientation, and other programming that helps us survive, people seem to have evolved to the point of possessing a considerable amount of free will; and I believe that God has gone to considerable lengths to assure this. It seems incongruous, then, to believe, as many people seem to, that God deprives them of freedom by imposing various plans and choices on their lives that they—somehow and for reasons that escape me—are bound to follow willy-nilly. "You play the hand you're dealt" means among other things that—whether or not God is the dealer—God doesn't play it for you.

* * *

Does God love you and me? It may well be that greater love hath not the Supreme Being than to give life to other beings and a beautiful world to live it in.

* * *

By loving other people, we love God. By receiving others' love, we receive God's love.

* * *

Perspective: The Sun, which is not large as stars go, has 313,000 times more mass than the Earth, yet the Earth seemed very large back while I was hitch-hiking a lot and even now during a long drive.

* * *

"First do no harm." Contrary to popular belief, these words were not part of the original Hippocratic Oath for physicians. They strike me, though, as being sound advice for everyone.

* * *

Children often ask why. So do other seekers.

Prayer

May we honor our Creator enough to respect all Creation and love all God's children as we love ourselves.

Really? This prayer, which reflects Jesus's Great Commandments, is within our own power to answer, hard as answering it may sometimes be.

* * *

What is prayer? For me it is talking to God. At first, it's a one-way conversation; but after a while, a good idea that I hadn't thought of may enter my mind. Is that God's answer? Or an answer of my best self, which may be a way that God answers?

* * *

Though there is a great tradition of praising God, I am more inclined to thank God.

* * *

Praising God gives credit where credit is due and may foster a fitting degree of humility within the praisers.

* * *

If, as I believe, a part of God is love, then perhaps a part of God (and of ourselves) is enriched when we love God as we're commanded to. Fear of God, on the other hand, may or may not help the person who fears, but I don't see that it helps God at all.

* * *

How does a person generate deep feelings of love for a Great Mystery? (Must one's love of God be felt?) I can't say it can't be done—zillions of people believe they feel it, and I suspect that for them God is not a mystery—but loving other people and treating them fairly and kindly is the most certain way I know for loving God.

* * *

We praise God when we appreciate, respect, and protect the world and creatures that God made.

* * *

We best love God, not by the fervor we may feel within ourselves, but by the compassion we show our neighbors and the consideration we show the Earth and all its creatures. We are, in a sense, God's guests on Earth and should conduct ourselves accordingly.

* * *

A prayer addressed to God sends a cc. to the most godly part of ourself. It addresses our best self, empowering us to an extent to answer our own prayers.

* * *

Best, I think, if we do not praise in order to flatter God or because we think God needs reassurance or that God's ego, if any, needs to be massaged by our prayers or hymns or cathedrals or flattering adjectives, or that God's favor can be bought. Rather, God deserves our praise and gratitude for all that God has done for us and everyone and everything else. Best case: praising God helps us to humble our own egos and so become better people by reminding us that we ultimately owe everything to God including our ability to do stuff for ourselves. Praising God reminds us, too, that there is a far greater Being above us, much as wearing yarmulkes is said to reminds Jews of the same. Our humility may please God, though not, I think, if we claim that we are miserable sinners, unless we actually are.

* * *

To put it a bit differently, we gregarious, community-minded humans may suppose that it's lonely being the one and only God. I doubt, though, that God has a fragile ego that feels hurt if we recent creations do not praise God adequately. It wouldn't surprise me, though, if God sees people who don't praise God as being rather limited in their outlooks. Nor can it flatter God for us to suppose that God rewards flatterers. I suspect that what pleases God more than praise, especially obsequious praise, is for us to feed the hungry, clothe the naked, visit the sick and imprisoned, and work to reform the status quo so that fewer people are hungry, naked, sick, or in prison. Or so Jesus said and I believe. (Matthew 25: 31-46)

* * *

Don Conover said, "Praying to God reminds us we are not alone."

* * *

Don again: "The particular way we come to find God's presence in our lives is not as relevant as that we do."

* * *

"O Lord, open thou my lips, and my mouth shall shew forth thy praise." (Psalm 51:15) But words without deeds vanish in the air. Better, I think: Open thou my heart, and my life shall show forth thy praise.

* * *

It is so much cheaper and more convenient to praise God in glorious song and earnest prayer than to feed the hungry, clothe the naked, and so on, and work for peace and justice.

* * *

We sometimes praise God with those mighty edifices of adjectives I've mentioned before—omnipotent, omniscient, et al.—moved perhaps by the same desire to praise and please that inspired the building of lofty cathedrals of stone and stained glass, which I'm glad were built. But God, I think, can no more be imprisoned in stone and glass than in lofty adjectives. Or by the sacred music that I hope God enjoys at least as much as I do.

* * *

If by any chance praising God helps to relieve God's loneliness (if any), then it's the least we can do for God after all God has done for us. As with Pascal's wager: if our praise helps God, so much the better; and if it doesn't, no harm done.[xiii]

* * *

Praying for trivial stuff trivializes prayer. Why bother God for a parking spot at the mall?

* * *

It seems that God has constituted us such that when we worship in a way that we are comfortable worshiping, we receive a peace that may be the peace of God.

* * *

Though I can seldom participate sincerely in receiving Eucharist, I admire and maybe envy the people who find peace by receiving it. As I watch the line of friends and strangers receive the bread and wine at the Weston Priory, I sometimes use the occasion to remind myself to try to make a useful difference however small. I find peace, though, in the silence of a Meeting for Worship or a snow-carpeted forest in winter or a desert in the sun, or in talking things over with Nancy or my children Erin and Brian or another

xiii Pascal's wager: Rationally we should live as though God exists, since if God does not exist, there's no harm done except maybe for a few pleasures foregone, whereas we invite damnation if God does exist and we live as though that weren't so.

loved one—all being gifts from God. Nancy feels closest to God when she's out in Nature.

* * *

Religious people who cling to the old creation myths thereby withhold from God the praise that is due to God for working the wonders of actual creation that the sciences are constantly uncovering, describing, and sometimes explaining. It's one thing to be grateful if God simply commanded things into being—"And God said, Let there be light; and there was light" and so on—as Chapter 1 of Genesis tells us. It's quite another to appreciate that God, though remaining largely unknowable, fashioned all things and creatures from the mysterious bursting forth of hydrogen and helium around 13.8 billion years ago.

* * *

When we allow ourselves to feel awe at a marvel like the Grand Canyon or Alaska's magnificent Denali, I think we are spontaneously praising their Creator. The same when we feel awe at an inspired work of art like Beethoven's Third Symphony (even though he wasn't a very nice person) or doubly so at the hymn of praise, "How Great Thou Art."

* * *

Praying for someone is a way of beaming one's love towards that person. I think it always helps, especially if the person knows that he or she is being prayed for. The prayers of other people helped me when I learned that members of the Priory community, some of whom I barely knew, were praying for me in 1999 during my vasculitis, which my doctor called a serious illness and, again, during my open-heart surgery and recovery in 2019. But, as we know, prayers often do not achieve the results prayed for; and as Adriana suggests below, prayers can be a cop-out from becoming involved and doing what's needed.

* * *

If prayers always "worked," people who live in communities like the Priory's that take prayer seriously would live far longer than everyone else.

* * *

Nancy's and my friend whom I'll call Sharon was in intensive care, hemorrhaging externally and internally. The doctors called the family into her room on two occasions when they feared she was dying. Nancy asked the Benedictine monks and some other people to pray for her; they and we and others did. Sharon stopped bleeding and stabilized. Cause and effect? But her illness didn't quit. Not long afterwards she sank beyond saving. After Jesus reportedly raised Lazarus from the dead, he presumably died later.

* * *

The power of prayer, when one person prays for another, is the power of love.

* * *

As Lou Gehrig was dying of the disease that bears his name, he told the assembled fans during his last visit to Yankee Stadium that he was the luckiest man alive. The gentle, humble, profound monk, brother Philip, knowing that he was dying of the same affliction and was being cared for most lovingly by his brothers, told them that he had never been so happy. My cousin Sue, surrounded on her deathbed by her sisters Laura and Doro, her brother Bill, and her partner Keith, kept telling them the joy she felt from their being together. Is this akin to the love that many people say enveloped them during a near-death experiences?

* * *

People often use prayer as a cop-out from taking the trouble or risk of actually helping people in need. On 9/11/1981, for instance, my friend Adriana lost two of her four daughters, her dad, and other loved ones to the terror in Guatemala (see "Peter" at pp. 83-84). They were all "disappeared" (kidnapped), probably tortured and killed, and were never heard of again. Later she and her surviving family fled through Mexico, crossed illegally into the U.S., and eventually entered the Sanctuary of a synagogue in Chicago, from which she spoke out—risking deportation back to the death squads that she had fled—in order to urge us Americans to do all that we could to end the U.S. support for the secret police who took her loved ones and most probably murdered them.

Of prayer, Adriana told me, "I've spoken at a lot of places where people have been moved to tears. They have cried, and they have come to me and said, 'I'm so sorry for what happened. I will pray for you.' That makes me really angry. I respect their religious beliefs, but we can't solve killings and disappearances and children dying of hunger with prayers. And they tell me, 'I'm very concerned about the situation, and I'm going to pray.' That's to do nothing about it. It makes you feel good. It's for your benefit. You are gaining your entrance in Heaven. People here [in the U.S.] are not willing to risk anything, not their comfort, nothing. 'I admire you so much,' they say, but they won't get involved."

* * *

Since God has given to us most generously, including a blessed ability to do a bit of God's work on Earth, it's only fair that we do what we can to follow God's way.

* * *

To praise God fully, let us see, study, and appreciate the marvels – so many of which we take for granted—of the world God has created. And stop despoiling them.

* * *

May the godliness within you and me help us to recognize new truth, sort old truth from error if we care to, and treat everyone with compassion.

Suffering

It's clear that God does not save all good people or their loved ones from suffering, sorrow, or early death. The Holocaust and the vast slaughters by Stalin and Mao happened. Nobody and nothing intervened to stop Jesus from being tortured to death.

* * *

If God loves us as we have been taught to believe, why do bad things happen to good people? No one knows how often God's interventions, suspected or unsuspected, may have blocked bad things, but obviously not always. Recognizing this reality demands more trust in God than many people muster, and so they give up their faith. Or else they bind up their wounds, reach a more realistic conception of mysterious God, and often receive a gift of peace.

* * *

How, we may ask, can we trust a God that allows our loved ones and ourselves to suffer pain, anguish, or early death? It seems not to be God's way to suspend the laws of physics and biology by which God causes our world to function, in order to always avoid human suffering. Rather, God leaves people and microbes free to do or oppose harm, and harm often wins. As we ponder suffering or endure it, we might remember to count our blessings.

* * *

As part of believing that God does not micromanage our lives, I believe that God does not choose to make us suffer. When chance or people or microbes or other hazards of God's Creation bring suffering, God is there to help us through if we avail ourselves of God's peace.

* * *

Much in the Bible encourages the erroneous belief that God always protects good and faithful people. Typically, these people live the best lives they can, see in all modesty that they are mostly doing so, and, WHAM, suffering befalls them. Then it may be only natural to blame God, be angry with God, or conclude that God does not exist. Some people, though, rethink their concept of the God. Two people who went through this process—God will protect me, God didn't, God is still with me though not as I had supposed— are Sister Dianna Ortiz (described at pages 16–17, above) and Rabbi Harold S. Kushner, who lost his son to a fatal disease and who, in 1981 published a popular book called *When Bad Things Happen to Good People*, which is still worth reading.[44]

But no explanation of why bad things happen to good people satisfies everyone.

* * *

Rabbi Kushner begins by saying, "There is only one question which really matters, why do bad things happen to good people? All other theological conversation is intellectually diverting...but ultimately without the capacity to reach people where they really care." He might, like Rabbi Hillel, have concluded that all other theological conversation is commentary.[45] Whether or not Rabbi Kushner overstates it, you probably see his point.

* * *

When tragedy brings on suffering, I think it must take *strength* to change one's concept of God, rather than giving up on God. Sister Dianna and Rabbi Kushner had the strength and humility to revise their faith. Do the rest of us? If we do, thanks be to God.

* * *

When catastrophe befalls, it may help to consider the folk wisdom that says, "You play the hand you're dealt." We may not choose the cards, but we can usually choose how to play them—to seize upon or create opportunities for ourselves, or simply throw in our hand. Consider Stephen Hawking and Christopher Reeve and other quadriplegics who persevered as long and admirably as they were able to.

* * *

Trusting God, if we can, helps to sustain us through bad times. That is a gift from God to us and from us to ourselves. "Though I walk through the valley of the shadow of death, I will fear no evil, for thou art with me. Thy rod and thy staff, they comfort me...." (Psalm 23) It's not that the evil won't befall me, but that I shan't fear it as it does befall me if I am able to maintain God's peace within myself. This is easily written in my warm, dry home.

* * *

It is so much easier to blame God than ourselves when we fail to try to prevent tragedy. How much less suffering would there be if good people were less passive? (They may be good, but they could be so much better.) And how good, actually, are people who remain passive as harm approaches? How preventable World War II was in the 1930s, probably with little or no violence, if German citizens or French and British rulers had stood their ground against Hitler's march to the inferno! It was common after that war to fault the so-called Good Germans who looked the other way while the smoke rose from the death camp ovens. But in part at least, those Germans got a bum rap. Yes, there was a time when they could have stopped Hitler without massive bloodshed, but later on, most Germans who opposed the Nazis faced prison or death. And it's not just the Germans, French, Brits, and the isolationist Americans of the 1920s and 1930s whose passivity allowed the Nazis to flourish. Sooner or later nearly everyone chooses whether to oppose what's harmful or dangerous or to look the other way.[xiv] My point is not to blame victims, but to encourage people not to join them.

* * *

The sense of justice that most children seem to be born with may be one of God's ways for reducing injustice and attendant suffering. How often that sense wanes as children mature!

* * *

To live is to learn pain, and pain often deepens one's life experience unless too much pain overwhelms it. In the same vein, the good feeling that comes with success may partly compensate for what we miss by winning, that is, the deepening of character that losing often bestows. I felt deep disappointment when I was passed over for partnership (i.e., let go) by the Wall Street law firm where I had toiled during eight years. But that failure freed me to be a better person and lead a better life (albeit with far less money) than I surely would have had had I received status and tenure at the law firm. I got lucky afterwards, but being let go opened the door for the luck to walk in.

* * *

Death is part of life. So is tragedy.

* * *

Old age is a war with many heroes and no survivors, but what a blessing it is to reach it! Each day is a gift, and the gift of life is magnificent. It certainly has been for Nancy and me. We are very grateful and hate to see our time here growing shorter. Carpe diem!

---

xiv This is not a recent concern of mine. In 1985, I dedicated my book, *The Turkey Shoot: Tracking the Attica Cover-up* to "the Good German. Everyone chooses whether to be one." Back then, I probably lacked sufficient compassion for the Good Germans of the years when opposing Hitler's evil invited one's own death.

Prophesy

A Biblical prophet was not a person who necessarily predicted the future but one who stood back from his society, pierced its received wisdom, saw the reality on the other side, and urged the society to make vital adjustments, however painfully. If today's prophets are doing their job as those prophets did back then, they are *always* voices crying in the wilderness and standing fast against the flow. If by chance they enter the mainstream, then it's time they move on, lest their gift of prophecy wither.

Proselytizing

There is much to be said for proselytizing so long as it is friendly, gentle, and not intrusive—which does *not* mean ineffective. The verbs would be "offer" and "explain," not "demand" or "expect." The process includes listening as well as speaking and the attitude of humility and openness to respecting the other person's point of view, conceding its merits (if any) and maybe admitting the superiority of parts of it.

* * *

One may persuade others by reason, love, humility, and example; or else not persuade them and, one hopes, respect the differences that remain. More likely than not, an argument is a discussion that nobody wins. The central beliefs of all major religions merit respect, if for no other reason than that so many good people believe them. Most heretics, like most other people, are usually doing the best they can.

* * *

Since God apparently invested a lot in preserving our free will, it seems wrong to try to impose our beliefs on other people, that is, to alter their chosen faith. If we can't persuade them with love, reason, humility, and example, then best we stop trying. It helps, of course, if we are free from believing there is only one path.

* * *

If we offer people what we consider a better way, it will help them and us if we have the humility to recognize that, in whole or in part, their way may be better than ours. For Christians, I'm thinking particularly of elements of Judaism, Islam, Taoism, and Native American beliefs.

* * *

I suspect that God, having apparently chosen to be mysterious, accepts diverse ways to worship, so long as people try to respect God and people, show compassion, and help the needy.

* * *

In converting souls, force, physical or otherwise, should be counterproductive.

* * *

During the Irish Potato Famine of the latter 1840s, when Ireland was still a British colony, an estimated million or more Irish people starved to death and another million fled their homeland. The British, out of their Christian compassion and wanting to do the Lord's work, would arrive in a village, heat a cauldron of soup over a fire, and invite the famished residents to dine if they first converted to Protestantism. Those who remained true to their Catholic faith continued to starve. Nancy and I sensed the hatred that lingered a hundred and sixty years later in the Irish guide who showed us a quaint little spot where soup saved converts.

* * *

The world has long needed an Eleventh Commandment, "Live and let live." Or, "Mind your own business. Butt out of other people's faith or lack thereof, sexual orientation, lifestyle, economic system, personal appearance, disgusting habits, or anything else that does not hurt you directly." Such a rule would have saved so many lives, avoided so much pain. It still would.

* * *

From a Quaker text: "...let us renounce for ourselves the power of any person over any other and, compelling no one, let us seek to lead others to Truth through love. Let us teach by being ourselves teachable.... Do you walk cheerfully over the world, answering that of God in everyone?"[46]

Sin

What is sin but needlessly hurting other people, ourselves, other creatures, or the Earth?

* * *

Sin may be doing what displeases God, but what is that? For me, it's unnecessarily hurting (or running a real risk of hurting). Why need it include anything else?

* * *

Is sin this simple? I answer, Yes—as long as we construe *hurt* broadly. So, get thee behind me, Satan. You're nothing but hurting personified. The word *sin* often makes the deed and the doer seem worse than they are.

* * *

If *sin* is simply needless hurting, is the abstract noun *evil* something more? I doubt it.

* * *

I do not believe that either sin or evil exists as a discrete entity or a mysterious abstraction. Rather, each results when people do as they wish heedless of the harm they inflict or risk inflicting on others. Or they yield to the perverse impulse that so many people seem to have (God knows why) to hurt people gratuitously. But *if* our words or deeds or thoughts do not cause harm, how can they be a sin? How can they be evil?

* * *

It follows that thoughts that obsess or misdirect us, thereby hurting us, are sinful. And other thoughts are not unless they lead to harm.

* * *

It is a cardinal sin to wield *sin* as a guilt-edged cudgel.

* * *

Wielding the sin cudgel often violates the aforementioned Eleventh Commandment, Live and let live.

* * *

Sin is often a straitjacket that others put on us until we learn to don it ourselves.

* * *

Sometimes, of course, hurting is necessary to achieve a greater good. Ask a surgeon or a dentist. Ask a person who rejects a lover. When it is necessary to hurt, it is equally necessary to hurt as little and gently as possible. Or *quickly* may sometimes be kinder than *gently*, as in tearing off a Band-Aid.

* * *

How can one talk about sin without sounding moralistic? Though I do not see the harm in sounding moralistic, many claim to, so I mostly try not to.

* * *

"The flesh is weak," we may say after doing something we know was wrong. But no, the flesh is strong, and we did not muster the strength to overcome its strength. The best way I know of to stop eating peanuts is to push the bowl away.

* * *

Saying "The devil made me do it" is far less pernicious than saying "God wanted me to do it." The former admits I'm wrong. The latter claims I'm too right to argue with.

* * *

Evil is the harm that commonly befalls when we pursue our own devices and desires heedless of the effect on others—inflicting poverty, pain, starvation wages, exploitation, insensitive remarks, and so on. Consider the robber, tyrant, or corporate executive who cares solely for material gain. They sin. What they do is evil. Because it hurts people. Consider, too, everyone connected with maintaining the slave trade and abusing its survivors and their progeny. Consider the ethnic cleansing of this Continent by our forebears, especially since there was, for many decades, sufficient land to share with the Native Americans who roamed or settled here millennia earlier. Consider my English forebears who spent centuries enjoying the fruits of Empire oblivious of, or indifferent to, the squalor, starvation, and carnage that they inflicted upon, among many others, my Irish forebears during centuries of brutal and exploitive occupation. During the Great Famine of 1845–1852,

> "thousands of shiploads of food were exported from Ireland to England while a million Irish people died of starvation.... When the need [for assistance] continued to be overwhelming, the British government abruptly ended all public relief assistance to Ireland."[47]

* * *

Those who exploit or oppress or ignore the poor both sin and insult the Creator of us all.

* * *

Is it a sin to tune out one's still small voice and refuse to heed the whispers of one's best self? If it leads to, or allows, hurt.

* * *

I suspect it's often a sin to assert that God said what God has not said.

* * *

Whatever is is natural.

* * *

Intolerance is not sufficiently credited with being the sin that it is, perhaps because many people are intolerant and some even feel righteous about it.

* * *

Same with impatience: Simply showing one's impatience may irritate one-self and whoever is within earshot, but I'd not call it a sin. Often though, American impatience is an obvious but never-tabulated killer on the roads. We hear that speeding kills, but never that drivers' impatience causes the speeding and tailgating that cause accidents, many of them fatal. It was such a relief to drive in Norway and rural France, where few speeded and nearly no one tailgated.

During the Covid pandemic that rampaged in 2020-2021, it was obvious but unquantifiable that simple, non-partisan impatience was a part of what drove many people to remove their masks or reopen their businesses and otherwise try to return to "normal" sooner than most medical authorities deemed prudent.

* * *

Since at least St. Augustine, people who killed themselves were customarily considered sinners, self-murderers, not to be buried in holy ground, and so on. In some faiths, they still are. For me, this treatment of these so-called sinners was and is a sin. I can think of few people more in need of God's love and our compassion than people who feel driven to take their own lives.

* * *

Is it a sin to habitually dominate the conversation, or simply a lapse of con-sideration for others? "A gentleman is never unintentionally rude," said Os-car Wilde. Nor is a lady.

* * *

Original Sin: Believing that what God made was good (Genesis 1) and knowing that I was born as God made me (as I evolved), I cannot believe that you and I were sinners from our babyhood—back when we were too incompetent to do anything except suck, smile, wail, pee, sleep, and poop—because some mythical couple ate a fruit that God told them not to in a mythical garden several millennia ago. (Four out of ten Americans are said to believe that this actually happened.) Yet the myth of Adam and Eve eating the forbidden fruit may alert us to the reality that we humans tend to hurt others, sometimes delighting in it; we may delude ourselves that we are not causing the pain we cause; and we need to be ever alert to our own perversity.

* * *

Original Sin: As we evolved (as God made us), we had such a capacity and sometimes tendency to harm each other that Jesus and other great prophets arrived, presumably inspired by God, to accelerate our moral evolution, so as to liberate our better angels and lead us to greater peace within and outside ourselves.

* * *

Original Sin: There are more than enough real sins—starting wars, hyping cigarettes and opioids, and so on—without clerics fabricating any more.

* * *

If there are intelligent beings on other planets, were they, too, born guilty of some Original Sin unless or until some Jesus came along to save them?

* * *

Original Sin is a myth that recognizes the darkness that ever threatens to overwhelm the godliness that is quietly illuminating the heart of each of us.

* * *

Hypothesis, doubtless not original, about the origin of Original Sin: Early theologians did not understand that God created us through evolution and mutations and survival of the fittest—that is, through a process in which imperfection is inherent. Instead, they faced the apparent quandary that perfect God could not have created anything imperfect; humans are obviously imperfect; this cannot be the fault of the perfect Creator; so it must be our own fault. Hence the theologians needed to create myths such as Original Sin and the Fall of Man. (Didn't Woman fall too?) Consider the scientists before Kepler who concluded erroneously that the perfect God must have caused the planets to swing around the Sun in perfectly circular orbits because God would not have created an imperfect solar system. Consider philosopher David Hume's failure to understand that an omnipotent Creator would not have created the imperfections that Hume perceived in Nature. (See page 10, above.)

* * *

"In a perfect universe," veteran science writer Dennis Overbye reported in 2020, "we would not exist."[48] Because, he explained, if the Big Bang had ended up producing equal amounts of matter and anti-matter, they would have annihilated each other, leaving nothing. Overbye, whom I greatly respect, seemed to assume that *perfect* means having equal amounts, which sounds like the folks who believed that the planets must orbit the sun in perfect circles. I dare say that a universe that annihilates itself at the get-go is far from perfect.

* * *

In law school we looked at what the legal Canons of Ethics prohibited, to see what lawyers were commonly doing wrong. The Ten Commandments give similar clues to common and serious human transgressions in Moses's day and ours.

* * *

I used to think that the Ten Commandments were harsh for saying that God visits "the iniquity of the fathers upon the children unto the third and fourth generation...." (Exodus 20:5) Finally, though, I realized that this is simply how things often work. Consider the price that we Americans are still paying for the enormous sins of our forebears in kidnapping and enslaving millions of Africans, and inflicting uncounted and unpunished assaults, rapes, and murders upon them, in the process of robbing them of their labor, their families, and their time on Earth.

* * *

How sinful it is to terrify and manipulate people by preaching that the God of love sends us into Hell to suffer the agonies of torture forever, to punish us for our alleged sins committed during our short lives. The U.S. imposes the longest prison sentences in the industrialized world; but God would impose endless years of torture? And make life without parole look like a romp in the park? That would make God an arch sinner, and I don't believe it. Rather, I expect that Hell may be being in the next life the person we make of ourselves in this one. So may Heaven.

* * *

Rewards of decency and wages of sin: We carry with us for as long as we exist in this life and the next (if there is one) the person that our thoughts, deeds, indulgences, sacrifices, and stuff we can't help have created within us.

* * *

It is a sin of our society to define *justice* as meaning only legal justice, so that we don't have to think about striving for the social and economic justice that everyone deserves but that would make rich people less rich—as they already are in Norway, for the most part quite contentedly.

* * *

Sin: Keeping the minimum wage below a living wage.

* * *

Is it a sin to take religion with great seriousness and certainty? Where religion holds undue sway, people tend to make mountains out of doctrinal molehills and sometimes kill their brothers and sisters in Christ over often insignificant differences. In several nations of western Asia, wearing the wrong garb can get a person killed. Where religion matters less, people seem less inclined to harm or kill each other over it.

* * *

Given Scripture's imperfections, is it a sin to question the soundness of any passage?

* * *

Attention America: Humility is not a sin. Neither is patience. I cannot say the same for instant gratification.

* * *

Tribalism: Consider that many French venerate Napoleon though he was several times a mass murderer.

* * *

Many deeds that are customarily called sins are not. Many deeds that are sins—because of the hurt they inflict—are curiously absent from the list. This seems particularly true for much sexual and business conduct. The same for criminal justice, so that people spend zillions of years in prison for deeds that are relatively harmless, whereas many deeds that cause great harm curiously escape prosecutorial attention or statutory mention. Many company executives knew that their cigarettes kill vast numbers, claimed they were safe, and secretly made them even more addictive; yet they are not serving life without parole. Same with the folks who caused the pandemic of opioid deaths. And those who brought on the 2008 financial crisis, and perpetrated fraudulent mortgage foreclosures, that threw millions out of their homes. As Jeffrey Reiman summed it up in the title of his 1979 classic, *The Rich Get Richer and the Poor Get Prison.*

* * *

Egregious and often unpunished violations of "thou shalt not steal" occur when rich people rob poor people, rich classes rob poor classes, rich nations rob poor nations.

* * *

Is it American's responsibility to aid the poor of the world? Of course. We have already accepted responsibility for exploiting them.

* * *

When we eat other animals, we are only doing what all carnivores do—though being omnivorous, we have a choice. When we are needlessly cruel to other animals—as factory farms, agribusiness, and slaughterhouses are often needlessly but profitably cruel—we sin.

* * *

Since workplace safety, like the responsible disposal of toxic wastes, cuts profits, it is often ignored, causing grievous harm or death to many people and no prison time for the executives who perpetrate these crimes.

* * *

Do not take the Lord's name in vain, says the Commandment. Habitually saying "Goddammit!" instead of some other expletive may hurt one's self by trivializing that which is most serious and sacred—whether or not it offends God. This, I think, is a lesser harm. A grand sin of taking the Lord's name in vain occurs when people claim that God approves of their torturing or murdering perceived heretics or anyone else, making wars, enslaving people, and so on, allegedly for God's sake. Thus we purport to enlist God as our accomplice in committing vile deeds. Thus we blaspheme as we sin.

Take the "Battle Hymn of the Republic." Its rousing melody probably makes it the most stirring song in our patriotic repertoire, but consider what its lyrics proclaim: that God took the side of the Union troops in the Civil War; that the killing and dying of hundreds of thousands of mostly young men was God's way of trampling out the grapes of wrath; that the men entering the abattoir were God's fateful lightning; and so forth. Confederate troops were, of course, equally certain that God was on their side.

Many will say that God was surely on the side of the Union's fight to end slavery. I doubt it. Even if we suppose (as I do) that God abhorred slavery, there is no reason for presuming that God wanted us to fight the bloodiest war in our history to end it. The Brits and their often-barbaric empire, the U.S. North, the Mexicans, and the Brazilians ended slavery without going to war. It may be fine to pray for God's guidance when we weigh questions of war and peace—recall that many Quakers felt led by their Inward Light to fight against Hitler—but it skews everything if we presume to thrust our own self-serving version of God's thumb onto the scales.

* * *

The fact that human slavery has existed through the ages and still exists does not mean that it was ever right. It's a sign that, even with the help of the great religions, human decency has evolved too slowly.

* * *

Any euphoria brought on by the notion of American exceptionalism may be tempered by recalling our nation's founding sins of slavery, ethnic cleansing, and the millions of resulting corpses that litter these centuries of sin.

* * *

Americans worship a Golden Calf, that is, the standard of living of the well-off Americans who, for the most part, run the country. And God forbid that anyone threaten the Middle Eastern oil or other resources that "we" "need" to maintain "our" standard of profligacy.

* * *

I think it's a sin to maintain an economy whose health requires constant growth in a finite world—a view that I suppose is still heresy.

* * *

Thou shalt not covet. The first nine Commandments tell us to do or not do various stuff. This one tells us, as a New Yorker might say, "Don't even think about it." As a boy I wondered why God would use up one of the ten on mere thoughts. But growing up in America showed me the answer readily enough. Hurt often results from entertaining a hot desire for our neighbor's house or spouse. Defying the Tenth Commandment, much of the advertising industry uses every trick in the book—a book the industry wrote—to seduce us into coveting, then buying more and fancier stuff than we need. Indeed, the health of our economy is said to depend on these seductions. So we have rampant materialism, overstuffed homes, a culture that unsustainably depletes resources, and a profligate lifestyle that pays lip service to God but homage to Mammon. Too many people squander their time and energy (= their lives) on the rat race for Velveeta cheese, then wonder where the satisfaction is hiding.

* * *

Capitalism need not be at odds with Christianity though it often is. I would say it's sinful to entice people to eat what's bad for them or more than is good for them, or to buy stuff they don't need or won't delight in, or to smoke what will kill many of them.[xv] *Thou shalt covet* is the marching order for the ads and commercials that relentlessly beset, irritate, insult, and deplete us.

* * *

Consider the automobile. Nothing wrong with owning a car; and the sounder and safer it's made, the better. Nancy and I own one. But TV ads for various cars and trucks give new meaning to the Commandments to have no other gods before God, to make no graven images, and not to covet. Often, through clever lighting and camera angles, the ad people display cars on TV as objects of adulation that would turn the Golden Calf green with envy. They stress the power and speed of cars and trucks as though prudent limits do not exist. Or stunt drivers (or computer simulators) slam a car or truck around some rocky outback—beat the shit out of their pricey toy—in ways that no sane person would treat his or her expensive machine, ostensibly to demonstrate that the vehicle can "take it," but more subtly to promote conspicuous consumption and create the illusion in male and some female drivers that they have big balls.

At least, automobiles' "annual model change" induces less needless buying than it used to; and the influx of better-made vehicles from Japan, Germany, et al. has made "planned obsolescence" somewhat obsolete, to the benefit the Earth and everyone on it.

* * *

Another price of coveting is the lottery ticket mentality: Many Americans who struggle to get by are conned or con themselves into believing that (a) they too can somehow strike it rich and (b) such luck provides their main chance (tiny) to no longer need to struggle financially. So they do zero to correct the System that exploits them, and that if corrected would obviate their need to dream of striking it rich. Again, consider Norway, where there are comparatively high taxes, little disparity in the amounts that people earn and own, little poverty or crime or drug abuse, and considerable contentment.

* * *

---

xv I believe this is not only a sin but also a crime that can and should be prosecuted under the various state reckless murder statutes. Cigarettes currently kill upwards of 450,000 Americans a year, 4.5 million a decade, in good measure through the lying, conniving, and secretly upping the power to addict by tobacco company executives who, in my judgment, should be serving life without parole.

God gave us life and a place to live it as best we can. It is a great sin to needlessly destroy either life or habitat.

* * *

If blessed are the peacemakers, then damned are the war-makers.

* * *

While starting a war is a monstrous crime, defending oneself is essential, and avoiding violence as far as possible is a sacred duty. Non-violence, though, may be the worse option when it permits violence to flourish, for instance in appeasing Hitler or not intervening to stop the slaughter of 800,000 people in Rwanda. I expect that many Quakers will disagree.

* * *

Self-defense being necessary for health or survival, aggressors commonly call their wars defensive, thus adding hypocrisy to their sin. One more reason *always* to scrutinize the Official Versions that the compliant U.S. media peddle about official U.S. violence.

The U.S. war against Grenada in 1983 was not defensive, nor was our 1989 war against Panama, nor was our 2001 war in Afghanistan (there were more "surgical" ways to deal with the Al Qaeda attackers there), nor was our 2003 war against Iraq.[xvi]

* * *

Citizens' passivity and omissions often hurt people needlessly, as when we go about our business while our government starts wars of choice (aggression), or abets murder and torture in other lands, or maintains brutal prisons here at home, or simply permits the massive pollution of land, sea, and air. Any reader can lengthen this list.

* * *

Sins of omission: People who leave it to God or to fervent prayer or to other people to tackle the ills of the world shirk not only their own responsibility to their sisters and brothers, but also their obligation to repay God, as best they can, for God's gifts to all of us.

* * *

"We have left undone those things that we ought to have done...." from "A General Confession" in *The Book of Common Prayer*.[49] Today's world is awash in sins of omission. Soon we may drown in them. For instance: lack

---

xvi Since the Constitution does not grant a President the right to start a war, the compliant U.S. media obligingly referred to the first two of these wars as "invasions." But if a violent invasion, conquest, and military occupation of these nations do not amount to war, what does? Media that are not compliant are often called "alternative media" and need to be treasured and heeded.

of urgently needed limits on population growth and on pollution of land, sea, and air; lack of laws, regulations, and enforcement sufficient to prevent the strong from exploiting, abusing, gouging, and poisoning most people; insufficient taxes to pay for a quality education and medical care for all and a just system of justice; fair distribution of the world's bounty, and other attributes of a civilized society. These are sins because they needlessly hurt and will hurt great numbers of people. They have been largely eliminated in several other nations. If little Norway can do it, why can't we?

* * *

Free will: We all enjoy, and many abuse, our freedom to turn a blind eye to much that needs to be seen.

* * *

Civil disobedience: Can obeying the law ever be a sin? Should we ever break the law in order to avoid committing a sin of indifference or passivity in the face of what we perceive as official wrongdoing? Where would civil rights be today without past civil disobedience? But the job isn't done; where will future civil rights be without more civil disobedience?

Consider the laws that enforced slavery and Jim Crow and have deprived citizens of their right to vote. The answer in each instance may depend on the heft of each option. The law is the backbone of good government. If someone breaks it, he or she must be ready to pay the price. What's worst is when the government breaks the law, as I'm afraid it often does. It has the physical force and, rightly or wrongly, claims the moral authority—the power and until recently, the trust. A government leads; a corrupt government corrupts. In fact, when the government becomes a lawbreaker, it may be immoral for individuals to obey the law. Consider Mahatma Gandhi and Martin Luther King, Jr., and their followers. They broke certain laws, but they were admirable.

This is a significant part of what faith in God *has* to mean. Sooner or later God's will, design, justice, higher law conflicts with the laws of humans, which are sometimes enacted for sinful purposes or, intentionally or not, have needlessly hurtful consequences. Then you make your choice. People *had* to break certain laws in Hitler's Germany in order to keep their integrity. That was true in this country during the long pestilence of slavery and Jim Crow, and it continues in various instances today. People choose to be guilty before the Establishment *or* before God. Or they look away, which is the easiest, most common, and perhaps most hurtful choice.

Soul

I am morally certain that the *me* of me is more than the flow of electrical or chemical impulses moving through the neurons of my brain and body. Rather, the body and its functions host and enable my soul during my so-called lifetime.

* * *

I suspect that our self-esteem helps us to conclude that each of us has a soul, however little the proof that we have one. Which does not mean we lack one.

* * *

The brain hosts the mind. The former is tangible and can be damaged. The latter, as far as we yet know, is intangible but can also be damaged. Does the mind shape the soul, or vice versa, or both, or neither? While brains and minds deteriorate, I believe that our souls are the essence of who we are and that they endure.

* * *

Does the soul develop as the body that hosts it develops? Do souls, like bodies, vary in size and abilities? Does an immortal soul exist, stunted if at all, in people who lack compassion? Clearly yes, in my Quakerly view; for our soul is where we hear, if we pause to listen, the godly bit that exists in even the worst of us. Recall the assurance that New York City's Fortune Society gives to convicted criminals, "You are better than the worst thing you have ever done."

* * *

People commonly assume that we humans are the only animals that have souls or immortal souls. Are we?

* * *

Many dog owners agree that people who don't love dogs exaggerate the difference between dogs and people. Is there That of God in a dog? How about in a dog that saves its master's life, especially by sacrificing its own? And in a cool or affectionate cat?

* * *

A common theory holds that a new human soul comes into being at the moment of conception or birth or some other specific time. But perhaps each soul already exists, and at some point, it pours into a vessel called a human body that then contains it and shapes it and serves as the vehicle by which it expresses itself. If so, does such a soul exist as an individual or as part of a common spirit or spirit pool before and perhaps after its temporary visit within a human body? Is it a reincarnation of a prior person? With the population exploding, there can't be enough old souls to supply all the new people unless maybe some souls come from other planets, or can be cut up and regenerate like a liver or a starfish. No joke.

* * *

It strikes me as most likely that the instant a sperm joins an ovum, they are *not* invested with a full-blown human soul. While conception starts a marvelous process, I suppose that a soul develops along with the embryo, fetus, baby, or child. Early on, that microscopic bundle of human cells does not have a heart or brain; why should it have a soul, and what organ would host one?

* * *

Whether a human soul evolves the way a human body does within the womb, or enters a person from some other place, or simply ignites at some point within an embryo, fetus, baby, or child, I do not know—and neither, I dare say, does anybody else. While it is uncomplicated and hence appealing to suppose that there's a full-blown human soul within the microscopic cells that exist the moment a sperm merges with an ovum—as many anti-abortionists assert with impenetrable certainty—nobody actually knows that this is so. Most probably it is not.

* * *

Putting it somewhat differently, I suspect that the moment a new human life begins may be the same moment that the equally unformed makings of its soul begin their equally lengthy development, but they won't be fully formed any sooner than their physical host is formed—and quite possibly even a newborn baby does not yet have a soul.

While a freshly inseminated ovum is human (adjective) as opposed to, say, bovine or feline, it has far to go before it becomes a human (noun).

* * *

While many people maintain the simple but unprovable view it's a human being at conception, the public dialogue seems curiously bare of voices saying, much more plausibly I believe, that it does not become a human being, hosting an immortal human soul, until later on. I'm surprised that "prochoice" advocates have not been pressing this argument.

* * *

Why would a newly inseminated human ovum have any more capacity to host a human soul than an amoeba has? The new little human life evolves mentally and perhaps spiritually, I suppose, during its stay in the womb and/or after it's born, into a soulful human being—much as a human body evolves in the womb, in a speedy miniature of evolution through the ages from early, one-celled animals. A five-month human preemie may look like a tiny baby, but is it truly a human being? Who actually knows? All we can say for sure is that if its life continues, it will most likely develop into a senior citizen.

* * *

Since anti-abortionists commonly rely on their certainty that the microscopic cells that exist at the moment conception harbor a human soul, these people should logically be angry at, or dismayed by, the relentless success of the world's leading abortionist, who happens to be Mother Nature, who aborts from 10% up to 40% of all human life that is conceived. Though we commonly call these events "miscarriages," the effect is the same death of what many people have come to call a "baby" that has been developing for days or weeks or months—and its death generally occurs for sound biological reasons.[xvii]

Why would a loving God place a soul in a bunch of human cells that stands about a 10% to 40% chance of dying through a "miscarriage," most during their first three months of development, some even later, before they become a real baby? If Mother Nature aborts all those fetuses for her reasons, why can't a human mother do the same without the interference of strangers, however well intended, who don't know her or her situation?

---

xvii According to the WebMD website, "In scientific terms, any pregnancy that ends before a baby is able to survive on its own is an abortion.... A spontaneous abortion is more commonly called a miscarriage. A miscarriage is the loss of a pregnancy before the 20th week. Miscarriages are common. But it's hard to know exactly how often they happen because many times it's before you've even missed a period or know you're pregnant. About 10%-20% of recognized pregnancies will end in a miscarriage. But researchers estimate the overall rate is closer to 40%.... More than 80% of miscarriages happen within the first 3 months of pregnancy.... Most miscarriages happen when the embryo or fetus has fatal genetic problems. Usually, these problems are not related to the mother.... At least 80% of women who have had a miscarriage go on to have normal pregnancies and births." Other respected websites roughly agree.

* * *

If as the Gospels of Matthew, Mark, and Luke tell us, the Holy Spirit descended upon Jesus when he encountered John the Baptist—in effect, that Jesus did not receive the Holy Spirit until he was an adult—then why would it be problematic for God to arrange for everyone else to receive immortal souls well after they are conceived? Indeed, I believe God arranges this.

I understand, too, that before the 19th Century, the Catholic Church did not claim that the human flesh within a woman's womb contained a human soul upon conception.

* * *

Back in the day, before pro-life P.R. replaced traditional terminology, the marvelous little bundle of life was not called a "baby" until after it was born.

* * *

Anti-abortionists and I agree that, sooner or later, each human being has a soul. An immortal soul? If so, does its immortality attach at conception when it's clearly not yet a person? Before a natural miscarriage? Before the human cells that host it learn to think or talk? Or does it become immortal at some point in the maturation of its host's brain or consciousness? Nobody knows, though many claim to know with a certainty that entitles them, they are also certain, to determine the welfare, morals, and health of women they have never met.

Forgiveness

Jesus said to forgive seventy times seven. (Matthew 18:21-22) Easier said than done, but it usually frees the person who does it.

* * *

A Benedictine nun in beleaguered Chiapas, Mexico, asked angrily in 1996, "How can you have reconciliation if there is no justice?" She was not alone. But after South Africa's apartheid regime ended, there was much reconciliation without punishment for those who confessed to the officially sanctioned tortures and murders they had committed. Forgiveness by the victims or their survivors (which was not universal) seems to have been a key to much peace and progress that followed. South Africa's Archbishop Desmond Tutu preached "No future without forgiveness" in the title and text of his book about his country's Truth and Reconciliation Commission, which achieved more of both than many had expected towards reducing the legacy of hatred bequeathed by South Africa's brutal practice of apartheid.[50]

* * *

Time and again in the American states that still use capital punishment, the execution of a convicted killer disappoints the victim's loved ones, who fail to feel the much-touted "closure" that conventional wisdom led them to expect. Neither revenge nor justice but forgiveness seems essential to any closure, however hard it may be to forgive. For what is closure except peace for the survivor?

* * *

We are told that once we forgive someone, the hurt we feel will be over and done. Not necessarily. Our anger at a person, and need to forgive, may arise and subside and rise again.

* * *

We are often told to forgive immediately. The Gospels suggest as much. But sincere forgiveness may take time, especially if one is not used to granting it. Indeed, trying to forgive rapidly may cause one to forgiving insincerely and so, ineffectively. Better slowly than falsely.

* * *

It is often said that before the victim can forgive, the wrongdoer must apologize. But waiting for that event, which often does not occur, keeps the victim bound to the decency of the wrongdoer. Good luck with that!

* * *

Forgiving people for their crimes does not mean declining to punish them— to put them for a time where they can't hurt anyone but fellow prisoners and to deter people who are capable of being deterred from committing crimes.

* * *

How do I forgive someone who hurt, not me, but a close friend? I finally realized that I had hardened my heart against (remained pissed off at) the perp, and the answer was obviously to soften my heart. I did so, promptly stopped pointlessly riling myself, and reopened myself to appreciating the good side of the perp and his accomplishments. The friend was Kevin Kelly. On his deathbed Kevin told the man who had hurt him that he forgave him, and the man wept.

Salvation

Why would the God that created everyone choose to "save" only a limited religious or tribal in-group? Countless people of several faiths are said to believe that God does this. I can't.

* * *

My supposition is that God has arranged for the *me* that leaves this life to be much like the *me* that enters the next, though hopefully free of physical and mental infirmities. If so, then people who have become compassionate and at peace may already be "saved."

* * *

Salvation means being saved from going to Hell? Or from reaping the wages of sin, which Paul said is a death (Romans 6:23), that is, being alienated from God?

* * *

Given the chancy ways that most people arrive at their beliefs, I cannot believe that God requires salvation in this life or the next to depend on the belief system, if any, that a person happens to espouse. We may be saved, not so much by what we believe as by what we do, or choose not to do, and we thus become.

* * *

Nor can I believe that God put us here to devote this life to focusing on the next. There's too much that needs doing here and now.

* * *

Focusing on one's personal salvation risks being, and often is, highly self-centered.

* * *

Holding that a person's salvation depends on believing a particular scenario about God, Jesus, et al. sounds less like the way that God acts than a human tactic to coerce people into religious conformity. But a faith founded on fear or force cannot be sincere. Does God really desire faux devotion? Or does salvation depend on freeing ourselves from the prison of the self, on showing compassion, doing selfless deeds, and developing into the person that results? Or?

* * *

Jesus saves to the extent that one becomes a better person by following his advice to love one's neighbor, show compassion, forgive as best one can, seek peace, and so on. He saves to the extent that he pointed the way towards saving ourselves. For each of us can, if we wish and persist, become our own savior at least in this life and, I suppose, in the next.

* * *

Espousing prescribed beliefs and practicing various rituals may move people towards salvation to the extent that these observances move them towards acts of compassion.

* * *

Doing deeds that help other people also helps to put the doer at peace. I suppose that God arranged it this way.

* * *

In sum, I suppose, like many others, that becoming good (godly) people here on Earth, happy and at peace, best prepares us for the next life if we get one. And I do believe we get one.

Hell

Traditional Christian doctrine, which many people still trust, has it that to punish you for stuff you did wrong on Earth, God will consign your soul to be tortured forever. So God is grossly more barbaric than Mississippi's Parchman Prison and New York City's Rikers Island were at their worst? That's not the God that Jesus usually taught and I believe in. But see Jesus's Parable of Sheep and Goats (Matthew 25:32–41).

Afterlife

The creation of a next world seems no more improbable than the creation of this one. The God who fashioned the Heavens and Earth and gave us life after birth most probably has the power to grant us life after death and may already have done so for legions gone. Or not.

* * *

If the God that gave us life also gives us an afterlife, so much the better; but it would be ungrateful to fault God if God does not—in which event, I assume I won't know it.

* * *

May God have ever said to God's self something like, "I went to all the trouble to create human beings and a corner of the cosmos that can sustain them, and the thanks I get from many of them is prayer after prayer for an endless nother life? Can't they be satisfied with all I gave them?"

Most people apparently want to keep on living after our time on Earth is done, though not in Hell, while resurrection of the body strikes me logistically difficult, not useful, and most unlikely—and maybe a concoction of people trying to deny our ultimate physical decomposition. I hope and believe, but am not certain, that we do continue after life on Earth. If so, what then? What form, if any, do we take? With what consciousness and abilities? Can we communicate with other souls? If so, how? Do language barriers remain; if so, may we learn other souls' languages?

* * *

Wonderful Heaven and awful Hell have served for ages as Christianity's carrot and stick to lure people into the faith and scare them into line. The canard that the God of all creation created a pit where people suffer the agonies of fire throughout eternity for the heinous sins they committed during their brief stay on Earth is not to be believed, at least not by me. Maintaining that God is a world-class torturer is no more realistic, I trust, than that God protects all good people from harm.

* * *

The fact that promises of an afterlife sometimes serve as instruments of exploitation or coercion does not prove that an afterlife does not exist. Neither does our natural desire to deny that death marks the end of us.

* * *

If there is no Hell, is there divine justice for people who get away with doing awful deeds on Earth? Do Stalin and Hitler enjoy impunity in an afterlife? Is it sufficient that evildoers must live with their awful selves presumably forever? Jesus taught that we should forgive "seventy times seven" (Matthew 18: 21-22), but he is also said to have said that people who do not feed the hungry, clothe the naked, and so on go to "everlasting fire." (Matthew 25: 31-46) The Koran speaks often of God's forgiving nature. Following the downfall of the white regime in South Africa and their murderous practice of apartheid, Nelson Mandela had the compassion and wisdom to forgive them; as mentioned before, Archbishop Desmond Tutu aptly summed it all up by naming his 1999 book about the Black regime's efforts at truth and reconciliation *No Future Without Forgiveness.*

* * *

According to Ta-Nehisi Coates, "Nothing in the record of human history argues for divine morality, and a great deal argues against it. What we know is that good people very often suffer terribly, while the perpetrators of horrific evil backstroke through all the pleasures of the world. There is no evidence that the score is ever evened in this life or any after. The barbarian Andrew Jackson rejoiced in mass murder, regaled in enslavement, and died a national hero...."[51]

Coates is right about justice in the life we know; but about justice hereafter, I see no evidence either way.

* * *

Pie in the sky by and by: The assurance of a heavenly afterlife has served for ages as a carrot to lull serfs, slaves, and similar exploitees towards accepting the stick—often the lash—of a miserable earthly reality. It will be ironic—some would say Divine justice—if in an afterlife, they end up happy and their oppressors, miserable.

* * *

Saying that Heaven and Hell are religion's carrot and stick does not prove that they don't exist. So do they? Only, I suspect, to the extent that we take into the next life, if there is one, the self-absorbed or compassionate person we are in this one.

* * *

In my experience, people who lead loving lives become better people than those who don't. I suppose that the former carry their virtues and self-improvements into the next life, though free from the impairments that may make them grouchy or mean or demented or deformed in this one.

* * *

The womb of Heaven or Hell is the small dark chamber located between our ears.

* * *

It may be all very well to say that salvation depends upon the grace of God—surely there can't be any salvation or life hereafter without God's wanting it—but this does not relieve us of responsibility for becoming the people we wish to be in this life and the next.

* * *

If Heaven and Hell do not exist per se, are good people nevertheless somehow segregated from bad people in an afterlife? I hope not.

* * *

In any next life, is there an opportunity to become a more compassionate and therefore happier soul? Can we free ourselves from the Purgatory of the self?

* * *

If we do not believe the Genesis myths or Gospel miracles and so on, must we also disbelieve in an afterlife? Of course not. The myths and miracles violate the laws of nature that God has laid down. As far as I can see, having a spiritual life after mortal death does not.

* * *

"Everybody wants to go to Heaven, but nobody wants to die," a prisoner famously scrawled on a death house door. For most of us, faith in an afterlife does not remove our eagerness to defer dying. If it did, it would defeat God's gift of life and presumed purpose in giving nearly all of us an instinct to cling to life as long as we reasonably can.

* * *

Nearly everyone has the ability to commit suicide, and a few do. Is it also possible to end it all in an afterlife if someone truly wants to? While killing oneself has been considered a sin or a crime, I truly hope that those who do it are embraced by love hereafter.

* * *

Nothing was explained to us when we entered this life except by parents and clerics who, many of us eventually realized, did not know as much as they may have believed they did. Yet many of us expect that somehow things will be explained as and when we enter a next life. That would be nice, I expect, if it happens.

* * *

What do we do for eternity? Without becoming eternally bored? The sound of a harp, even an Irish harp, grows quickly old. Since we presumably have no need to eat, reproduce, earn a living, or seek peace and justice in a Hereafter, does time drag? How does one while away the minutes and millennia of eternity? Does time exist? Are there challenges to meet, learning to be had, ways to find and communicate with the souls of people we loved or knew or wanted to meet, or with our forebears? With Siddhartha Gautama, Saint Augustine, Abe Lincoln, F. Scott Fitzgerald, or my great grandfather George Stoddard who died in a Confederate prison at, I'm told, the age of twenty-two? Can I read all the books I'll never have time for here? Can people who were illiterate learn to read? Can Nancy be my afterlife's companion?

* * *

One day I speculated that the way time exists in the hereafter may differ from the way it exists here. A friend replied, "Maybe there's only NOW." So maybe after Omar Khayyam died, he changed his tune: "The moving finger writes, and, having writ, stays put."

* * *

In an afterlife, do people's souls ever sleep? Do days and nights exist? Being awake 24/7 in this life is hard mentally as well as physically. Is it hard there?

Is time still linear? It may be that in an afterlife, time does not exist or exists very differently from the way we experience it now. Same for our individuality.

Will life in an afterlife be as incomprehensible as life and God are now? Will clerical souls create dogmas and explain them to our souls?

May our values change? Can we imagine a Heaven without a shopping mall?

Whatever else one says about life on Earth, it is *very* interesting. I cannot believe that the next, if any, will be an eternal bore. That would be Hell.

* * *

If God is as ubiquitous as we told, then God is present not only on this little planet but throughout all the stars and comets and planets and other matter strewn across the billions of light years of the cosmos. Do we learn more about God after we die than the little we know today? Do we meet such a

Being? Or meet Jesus? Or meet the souls of intelligent beings from other planets? Or some angel or other savvy spirit who explains things in a way that we shall understand? Can we somehow be with God? How could one be with a Being that is everywhere across all the billions of galaxies? God may well be vast enough to be able to cuddle billions of souls one by one from planet Earth, but for how long, and then what?

* * *

"Let the words of my mouth, and the meditations of my heart be acceptable in thy sight, O LORD, my strength, and my redeemer." Psalm 19: 14. I consider it fortunate that while the words of my mouth are available to anyone within earshot, only God may know the meditations of my heart, some of which would hurt or piss off several people if they knew them. Does this arrangement hold in the afterlife? Can we keep our secrets to ourselves hereafter? Or may everyone divine what everyone else is thinking?

* * *

And if we humans continue, what, if any, other animals continue? And what do *they* do forever? Do predators enjoy the proverbial Happy Hunting Ground? If so, what about their prey? I suppose that if we don't get an afterlife, no other animals do either. How about extraterrestrial beings that are significantly more advanced than we are?

* * *

I have been told, but doubt, that the Resurrection of Jesus is the key to Christianity; and if one doesn't believe it happened, then one isn't a Christian. For me, the Gospels' accounts of the Resurrection are encouraging but not convincing as to whether we shall continue as discrete individuals after we depart this mortal life. We may hope the Gospels were right about this, but we know they erred about some things; we suspect they erred about others.

* * *

Evidence for an afterlife: 1. Biblical accounts. 2. Many people's near-death experiences, which neurological explanations may or may not explain away. 3. Many people have been sure they felt the presence of someone who has died. But for me, the current state of the evidence is not conclusive. If that matters.

* * *

A very sensible friend told me that a psychic had enabled her to communicate with her husband, who had died of Alzheimer's, and he was no longer burdened with that impairment.

* * *

Various scientists claim to have explained away the near-death experiences that many people feel they've had. Typically the scientists say, "You did not go through a tunnel or see a bright light or meet departed loved ones during the time that your heart and brain flatlined; all this was simply an illusion that your dying brain created." But why would all those dying brains conjure up the same plausible scenario—often without knowing that many other people have reported the same—unless they or their souls actually experienced it? May not the dying brain, which some scientists find conclusive, have actually been the vehicles or pathways or means by which these people experienced beyond-life reality?

* * *

Some people, Nancy and my son Brian for instance, have reported that they perceived the presence and received a message from someone who has died—her father and my mother, for instance. How does this happen? Atheist scientists probably have an explanation that I probably won't believe.

* * *

While I have no opinion as to whether people have special angels who sometimes help them out, I have sensed now and then since my mother died that she brought me a stroke of "luck" that I hadn't expected. When I mentioned this to several friends, one replied that he had had the same sense about his departed mother. Another said the same about his father. When this happens to me, I say in my head, "Thank you, Mother."

* * *

People who survive near-death experiences often report that they reunited with loved ones who had passed before them. If this indeed happens, then whom do unwanted children who grew up in orphanages unite with? One hopes it's with some form of God's enveloping love. Then there was the bishop, being assured on his death bed that he'd soon be meeting his loved ones, growled, "I hope it's more than just a damn family reunion."

* * *

My father was Phi Beta Kappa at Harvard College and made the *Harvard Law Review*, which only the best students do. For as long as I knew him, he was always reading one book or another or the latest issue of *Foreign Affairs* or *Time* magazine. Among the thoughts flooded through me after the heart attack took him at the age of eighty-five, I supposed at the time that all the information and knowledge and wisdom that his mind had so wonderfully retained over his lifetime were turning into mush along with his brain. But if the person we have become accompanies us into an afterlife, don't our knowledge and understanding and compassion come along too? If they do, will they enrich our afterlife as they enrich us while we live? All the more reason to study in school, read, travel if possible, and lead a full life.

* * *

Did human life really rekindle within Jesus's battered, punctured body shortly after he was tortured to death? I doubt it. If it did, where did it go? Did its atoms become insubstantial and vanish like dust in the wind? Did it still eat, pee, and deteriorate as it aged? But did his spiritual presence appear to his disciples as we are told in the Bible? Since Nancy and Brian could sense my mother, surely they *could* sense him.

* * *

I cannot believe that our fate in a next life depends on which creed or holy narrative we espouse in this one.

* * *

The debate over the importance of beliefs versus works ended, for me, when I considered the serene feeling of peace that doing a good deed brings me. Carrying that peace into an afterlife may be what going to Heaven means. But I have never experienced peace from a creed.

* * *

If the nature of our Heaven depends on the person we have become by the time we die, then the niceties of the religious doctrine that we may or may not espouse probably matter little. Surely it matters too little to have fought wars and roasted heretics over. How ungodly!

* * *

If there is an afterlife in which we continue as individual souls and if, as seems likely, it happens in an immaterial venue, then how satisfying can it be for people whose joys on Earth were material—fancy house, overpowered car, shopping, astute investments, remodeled kitchen?

* * *

Why just one afterlife? Maybe there's reincarnation into another life on Earth or on another planet or in another cosmos, or an afterlife after an afterlife. We know so little.

* * *

If God grants us an afterlife, is it eternal? Would we want it to be? That's hard to answer unless we know what it's like. Do our wishes matter? As far as we know, they didn't when it came to being born. We are often told to be careful what we wish for.

* * *

Whence and why arose the traditions that ghosts mean to hurt us, not help us or simply say hello?

* * *

We speak of everlasting life, eternal life, and so on; but suppose that in a next life, time as we know it does not exist? Without time, what is eternity?

* * *

The Sun is predicted to blow up in about five billion years to a size and intensity that will envelop Mercury and incinerate everything that's combustible on Venus and Earth. If there is an afterlife, will it end then? Or continue thereafter? Do we really want to live even that long? Or does an afterlife exist outside of time and space?

* * *

As I recall, it was in 1948 when I was sixteen—"underage"—and my friend Jim Keller and I were having an illegal drink in Armando's on Montague Street in Brooklyn, that I told him that since God has given us a wonderful life, I trusted that God does right about an afterlife for humans, whatever that is or isn't. As you've seen, this trust in God is the same now as it was then. And, happily, Jim and I remain friends.

* * *

Whether one believes in the Resurrection of Jesus or an afterlife for oneself, we can't do anything about them. Jesus returned in some form or he didn't. We continue or we don't. What we can control is whether we follow Jesus's teachings and example here and now and become the person we wish to carry into the next one—whether or not it exists.

* * *

Is one life sufficient, even a long one? Each day is a blessing, and I can't help wanting more.

* * *

Earth provides plenty to do. Does Heaven?

* * *

What may life be like in an afterlife? We shall cease or we shall see.

War

A few more words about my bias here: The traditional peace churches are Church of the Brethren, Mennonites, and the Religious Society of Friends; there are others. In fact, Quakers are not as absolutely committed to peace and non-violence as many people suppose; during World War II individual Friends were all over the spectrum. Some went to prison (or not) as conscientious objectors, some did alternative service, some obtained non-combat assignments in the armed forces, and some fought. As mentioned in "Jews," if I had been a Quaker and old enough back then, I would have been among the many Friends who joined the military to stop the Nazis.

Consider the vast sacrilege of war, the willful smashing of God's living temples.

* * *

During my youth and middle age, I played lots of tennis. Memorable events in my life include sitting in the grandstands at New Haven, Connecticut; Stratton Mountain, Vermont; the U.S. Open in Flushing Meadows, New York; and once at Wimbledon several miles south of London. A favorite pastime has been and remains watching Grand Slam tennis on television. As I watch, I sometimes think that under other circumstances, fine young Germans like Boris Becker and Steffi Graff or Russians like Maria Sharapova and Daniil Medvedev would be killing and being killed by us Americans. What a waste! For what? How stupid!

* * *

In his book *How We Die*, a thoughtful surgeon named Sherwin Nuland noted that "85 percent of our aging population will succumb to the complications of one of only seven major entities [coronary artery disease, hypertension, cancer, etc.].…. These seven make up the posse that hunts down and kills the elderly among us. For the vast majority of those of us who live beyond middle age, they are the horsemen of death."[52]

The horsemen comprising this posse have changed slightly over the three decades since Dr. Nuland wrote this, but their relentlessness has not. Today we may note that a determined posse is riding in hot pursuit of humankind. Its horsemen include:

Climate change: We are told that if you put a frog in a pot of water and raise the heat slowly, the frog will sit there until it's cooked. I don't know if this is true of frogs, but it is clearly true of climate-change deniers.

Epidemics: We have been living through a Golden Age where one drug or another could cure many diseases. The Age is ending, thanks to (1) the profligate use of antibiotics for fattening cheap meat, (2) doctors who facilely prescribe antibiotics to cure the sniffles, and (3) the paucity of government-funded research whose goals do not depend on the prospects of turning quick profits that attract Big Pharma's research. As the Age wanes, germ-carrying jet travelers speed its demise and, too often, ours. The Covid-19 pandemic is the latest but surely not the last instance.

People explosion: This is a no-brainer that leaders with no brains or courage continue to ignore at everybody's peril. Whatever the point of life is, it is not to load the planet with as many people as possible. Billions too many are here already.

Things explosion: Our addiction to economic growth is as insane as population growth, the main difference being that the high priests of economics peddle the myth that the former is essential to economic health.

The U.S. lifestyle: As the world's resources dwindle, the U.S. stands ready to defend to the death the physical comforts of the middle and upper classes. It has made wars in the Middle East to keep the oil flowing. Victory in the 1991 Gulf War may have enabled the air-conditioners to keep running for a while in the cars of the folks who can afford them.

Victory of the rich: The One Percent have won the struggle for wealth and are mopping up isolated pockets of resistance. Prepare the guillotine. The deluge that Louis XV is said to have foreseen in France circa 1757 impends in America.

Human nature. In prehistoric times tribes presumably needed aggressive leaders to survive. Today it's still the aggressive who get to lead—Vladimir Putin, Margaret Thatcher, Kim Jong-un, Xi Jinping. What contented person would want the job of being the U.S. President? Until recently, though, aggressive leaders caused wars that killed merely thousands or millions. But science has evolved faster than human nature, world leaders remain as aggressive and ignorant of unintended consequences as ever, and the Nuclear Age threatens to be rather short.

Nuclear war: The U.S. and Russia have roughly 7,000 nuclear weapons apiece and on very short notice can launch a great many of them at each other. This has nearly happened several times. By accident or design or the impulse of an unstable leader, the end of life may begin at any time and surely will at some time unless these two idiot nations plus China, North Korea and the other "nuclear powers" stand down.

* * *

What I am about to say regarding the Golden Rule may sound harsh because (a) it is, and (b) thanks to omissions by the mainstream media and most schools, Americans are largely unaware of the harsh conduct by which our government advances U.S. interests abroad. So:

During the terrorist attack of 9/11/01, a handful of Middle Easterners finally did unto the United States what the United States has long been doing or abetting—by coups, military advisors, training, weapons, etc.—unto the people of Iraq, Iran, Egypt, Nicaragua, Honduras, the Philippines, the Dominican Republic, El Salvador, Panama, Bolivia, Brazil, Indonesia, Chile, Guatemala, Vietnam, et al. We have caused, or been instrumental in causing, several of these nations to endure many times more deaths than we endured on 9/11—¼ million in Guatemala and El Salvador, ½ million in Indonesia, and so on. Our lives are too short to ponder one by one those ¼ and ½ million souls and their bereaved loved ones.

During the days after the Twin Towers went down, we heard poignant stories about the relatives of the nearly 3,000 vanished souls who went searching through the shadowed canyons of lower Manhattan in the vain hope that *their* loved ones had somehow survived; and I thought of my friend Adriana Portillo-Bartow riding bus after bus to the end of the line time after time in Guatemala City, looking out the window for her two young daughters whom the U.S.-backed security forces had "disappeared" on the same day that they seized her dad (see "Peter," pp. 83–84), which happened to be on 9/11 of 1981.

* * *

Reportedly, an Egyptian surgeon named Ayman al-Zawahiri, who had been radicalized by being tortured by the U.S.-backed Egyptian government, wanted to overthrow that government; but Osama bin Laden thought it would be more effective to attack, not this "near enemy," but the "far enemy," meaning us, whom he saw as propping up the Middle Eastern status quo.[53] Bin Laden prevailed, and, *voila*, 9/11. But considering the vast numbers of people that U.S. wars, tortures, and support for repressive regimes have caused to hate us, I would say it was mere chance that led those Arabs rather than, say, Guatemalans or Salvadorans to fly those airliners into the Twin Towers and the Pentagon.

* * *

Tolerance, forgiveness, and non-violence among nations used to be optional. No longer.

* *

The Dalai Lama has suggested that "world leaders meet about once a year in a beautiful place without any business, just to get to know each other as human beings."[54] How sensible yet unlikely!

* *

Louis Menand, who teaches at Harvard, wrote in his review of Eric Schlosser's 2013 book, *Command and Control: Nuclear Weapons, the Damascus Accident, and the Illusion of Safety*:

> The American nuclear war plan, known as the Single Integrated Operational Plan (SIOP), provided for only one kind of response to an attack: full-scale nuclear war. It was assumed that tens of millions of people would die. There were no post-attack plans. For forty years, this was the American nuclear option. No doubt, the Soviets' was identical.
>
> Henry Kissinger called the SIOP "a horror strategy." Even Nixon was appalled by it. Schlosser says that when General George Butler became the head of the Strategic Air Command in 1991 and read the SIOP, he was stunned. "This was the single most absurd and irresponsible document I had ever reviewed in my life," he told Schlosser. "I came to fully appreciate the truth.... We escaped the Cold War without a nuclear holocaust by some combination of skill, luck, and divine intervention, and I suspect the latter in greatest proportion."

Who can disagree? Helpful if Schlosser's book had been a bestseller, but it wasn't. Dr. Menand concluded his review:

> In the end, the Soviet Union gave up, something that no one had predicted. But today many smaller powers have nuclear weapons, and even in the unlikely event that no leader of one of those nations ever decides to use them, out of fear or anger or insanity, there is always the possibility—*in the long run, there is the inevitability*—*of an accident.*[55]

My italics. Who can disagree?
Not to mention that the U.S. and Russia still have those several thousand

nukes pointed at each other and ready to "launch on warning."

From "Nuclear Weapons or Democracy" by Craig Lambert in *Harvard Magazine*:

> An exchange that exploded as little as 0.015% of the world's nuclear arsenal—say, between lesser nuclear powers like India and Pakistan—could leave 44 million dead immediately—and one billion more people likely to perish in the following month, given the effect on food supply and the disruption of agriculture.[56]

During the 1974 impeachment proceedings of Richard Nixon, he told the press, "I can go into my office and pick up the telephone, and in 25 minutes 70 million people will be dead."

Eighteen *Ohio* class submarines armed with nuclear ballistic or guided missiles patrol the world's waters. Their armaments can destroy all human, animal, and plant life on a continent.... Eight new [*Ohio* class submarines] were launched between 1989 and 1997, during the years of the so-called "peace dividend.".... Twelve more *Ohio* class submarines are slated for construction between 2019 and 2025.

* * *

In a 2005 *Foreign Policy* essay, 'Apocalypse Soon,' [former Secretary of Defense] Robert McNamara declared, "U.S. nuclear weapons policy [is] immoral, illegal, militarily unnecessary and dreadfully dangerous."[57]

* * *

President Dwight Eisenhower on the advent of nuclear war with the Soviets: "You might as well go out and shoot everyone you see and then shoot yourself."[58]

* * *

An editorial in the July 4–17, 2014, *National Catholic Reporter* concluded:

> President John Kennedy captured the gist of the matter 53 years ago, when he spoke about a "nuclear sword of Damocles, hanging by the slenderest of threads, capable of being cut at any moment by accident, or miscalculation, or by madness." That sword still hangs—and we still live in a world of accidents and miscalculations, a world still capable of madness.

* * *

The profound George Kennan: "I have no hope that a nuclear disaster can be avoided."[59]

* * *

Back in "Science" (p. 32), I advocated teaching basic astronomy and biology in Sunday schools so that youngsters may appreciate what God has created and thank God for it. Physics Professor Michael Pravica gave a more urgent reason for teaching science to everyone: "Given the reality that nuclear weapons are likely here to stay, what is...worrisome is that our leaders are in general scientifically illiterate and thus honestly wouldn't have a clue as to the terrible destructive potential of these weapons of mass destruction for all life on this planet."[60]

* * *

Another reason to believe there's intelligent life on other planets: God seems to favor intelligent beings or God would not have created us as, I believe, the highest form of life on Earth. But I doubt that God would have put all God's eggs in one basket by creating such beings only on Earth, especially since God probably knew that we'd become smart enough to figure out how to end all life but remain dumb enough to maybe do it.

* * *

It's a rare leader who will "back down" or risk "looking foolish" in order to avoid a war. Abraham Lincoln was such a person. So was Mikhail Gorbachev. And who today?

* * *

"Compassion is the pillar of world peace."
                                        —His Holiness the Dalai Lama[61]

* * *

Will God intervene to prevent the owners of nuclear-tipped missiles from destroying life on Earth? Like General Butler, I think God has already intervened, maybe several times. Will God keep it up? I doubt it. Consider the vast slaughters that God did not prevent in the 20th Century alone. I find it incomprehensible that the leaders of the nuclear powers have not put their temporary differences aside and done *whatever* it takes to sensibly avoid the ultimate disaster. A word to the wise is said to be sufficient, but the fate of humankind rests with fools, meaning the august heads of state who have not bothered to make nuclear disarmament their top priority.

Counting on divine intervention to avert tragedy is an evasion that courts disaster. Averting tragedy is our responsibility, not God's. Blessed are the peacemakers? Vital are the peacemakers!

* * *

In a book called *The Faith Instinct: How Religion Evolved and Why It Endures*, a *New York Times* science and editorial writer named Nicholas Wade wrote much about the history, nature, and uses or religion over the past 50,000 years.[62] His main argument was that during the Darwinian days of frequent tribal warfare, the fittest tribes, those whose warriors were willing to fight fanatically and die for them, generally survived by killing off the less fit (more rational?) tribes. Tribes that somehow had religious genes produced these superior fighters. It didn't matter what the religion was, Wade held, so long as it employed rituals, drumbeats, dances, and chants that worked its fighters into frenzies.[xviii] So religion served war, and war served human evolution. Not the message of the Prince of Peace.

However much truth there was in Wade's argument—possibly a lot, I suppose—it is not true today. The God of the Old Testament may have been a God of war, but the God of Jesus and the New Testament is a God of peace, though many wars have been fought in this God's name.

* * *

Once upon a time, war may have advanced civilization. Today it imperils it. Duh!

* * *

War: a game in which nations kill off each other's youngsters until nobody wins.

* * *

Do we suppose that all of the millions of people we have caused to hate us lack the will and skill to acquire and use a nuclear weapon? In medieval England and Wales, wily attackers sometimes captured dauntingly fortified castles—moats, thick stonewalls, portcullises, and so on—by simply bribing the guards. Who is to say that wily terrorists won't use this age-old tactic to obtain a nuclear bomb or two? Then suppose that an unattributed explosion wipes out Moscow. Who is to say that the surviving Russians will not retaliate against Washington? Or vice versa if Washington vanishes under an unsourced explosion? One more reason it's folly not to dismantle all nuclear weapons and, paraphrasing Reagan, "trust but verify" that it's been done.

* * *

They say that suicide is a permanent solution to a temporary problem. So is

---

xviii In a secular equivalent, I felt invincible while marching with fellow soldiers in the mid-1950s to the blare and beat of a military band. During bayonet training, we were taught to shout that we were killers and growl savagely while thrusting. All in the good cause du jour, no doubt.

nuclear war.

* * *

A common delusion, and a perilous way to violate the Commandment against taking God's name vain, is to claim that God is on "our side" in a war. Jesus and other enlightened people teach that God is on the side of peace.

* * *

My old friend Rev. James Parker Keller in 1988:

> Dare we live on the resurrection side of the cross, where life and peace are what we proclaim and live by, or are we still trapped on the crucifixion side? The Romans used crucifixion to punish anyone who dared to defy their authority, and even those suspected of being disloyal. The Romans believed that military force, punishment, and death [were] the only language people who disagreed with them understood.... The military solutions being used in Central America—and in many other places—no matter how disguised, are a form of crucifixion. Dare we say, because of the resurrection, that there is another power that can bring about peace? Dare we live by that power, and call upon all the nations of the world to do so?[63]

* * *

It has been common wisdom since Machiavelli that a mighty nation was safer being feared than loved. But those days ended on 9/11, when nineteen young men out of the multitude whom U.S. conduct has provoked into hating us demonstrated that the most determined and resourceful of them can and will hurt us. As never before, our lives and the lives of our children depend on reducing America's readiness to make wars, intervene violently, support tyrannies, and thus provoke people into giving up their lives in their passion to hurt us.

* * *

Followers of Jesus and the other prophets have not yet brought people to live together as the brothers and sisters that we are. Through Jesus's teaching and example, God tried love, and it hasn't worked all that well. Terror may do it. If it doesn't, so much for the experiment called life on Earth. And a star rose in the West over Alamogordo, New Mexico.[xix]

---

xix Alamogordo was the site of the first nuclear explosion. The second was on Hiroshima, the third on Nagasaki.

* * *

Will you, dear reader, join me in a modest step towards peace and fellow-ship? "The Battle Hymn of the Republic" may be the most rousing tune in many Christian hymnals and indeed in our whole patriotic repertoire, yet it glorifies a war and an Old Testament God that supposedly sought justice by killing people, whereas, as noted in the chapter on Sin, I think God would have preferred to end slavery without the vast internecine slaughter called the Civil War.

So I wrote new words for this stirring music, three short, patriotic verses that embrace everyone of every color starting with the Native Americans who got here first.[xx] I called this anthem "Walk in Freedom" and placed it in the public domain so anyone can use it free. I now offer it to you in Appendix B. Might the people in your church, synagogue, school, or other meeting place like to sing it? Want to give it a try? Or copy and publish it? If so, go for it!

---

xx I wrote about all this at greater length, and placed the lyrics in the public domain, in an article called "A Modest Step towards Peace and Union" in the July 2008 issue of *Friends Journal: Quaker Thought and Life Today.*

Practice

The Religious Society of Friends has divided itself into geographic regions, each of which has its own guidebook called Faith and Practice.[xxi] *Each book is written by the Quakers of that region upon reflection and discussion and their knowledge of the Quaker Way; each has much in common with the books of the other regions, though also sharp and sometimes basic differences. While Quakers have no formal creed, the* Faith *part of these books records examples of what other Quakers have thought, believed, and written over the three and three-quarters centuries since we began; the* Practice *part sets out the procedures that Quaker Meetings of the region are advised to follow regarding membership, the conduct of Meeting business, marriages, and so on.*

Applying the scheme of those books to this book, all that has gone before are reflections on Faith. *Now come my reflections on* Practice, *though they are not so much a set of procedures as they are thoughts on what needs doing or not doing. Whereas the* Practice *sections of the Quaker books tell one all one needs to know to be a practicing Quaker—which isn't much—the following pages offer only a few of the zillion ways there are to lead a godly life. Paradoxically perhaps, many suggested practices probably sound like principles.*

The Earth was here before we were born and will remain, rather the worse for wear, after we depart. In arranging Creation to evolve us to our present state, God entrusted us, as Genesis presciently said, with power over the Earth and much of what's on it—to share not own, to nurture not pillage, to take what we need and restore what we can. This much we owe to our Creator and fellow creatures and progeny. Yet it is a debt that many millions of people ignore as obliviously as though they were still three years old.

---

xxi Such a region is commonly called a "yearly meeting," signifying that the Quakers within it hold their "meetings for worship with a concern for business" (business meetings) once a year, e.g., New England Yearly Meeting, Philadelphia Yearly Meeting, Indiana Yearly Meeting. Yearly meetings are commonly divided into quarterly meetings, so called because they hold their business meetings four times a year. Thus a yearly meeting may comprise more or fewer than four quarterly meetings. Each quarterly meeting, in turn, comprises several monthly meetings, that is, local Quaker congregations, which commonly meet for business once a month and for worship every First Day (Sunday). One joins the Religious Society of Friends by joining a monthly Meeting. Readers interested in contrasting Faith and Practice books might go on line and compare those for New England and Indiana Yearly Meetings. These books commonly contain advices and queries for the Meetings in the region.

* * *

As a practical matter, love is the key that opens up the real world, that is, God's world. Love gives warmth and purpose to reality. I believe in the palpable power of love as a force that operates in our world, and that prayers that express our loving concern for one another are sometimes answered. Answered or not, they broaden the one who prays.

* * *

Consider how many of our ancestors probably died during the travail of giving birth to the next generation of our ancestors. We may express our gratitude to all those mothers by doing the best we can for succeeding generations. Like ceasing to pillage and pollute the Earth and stanching the explosion of population and merchandise. Neither the people nor the planet benefit from crowding as many of the former as possible onto the latter.

* * *

The love and support in which the brothers of the Weston Priory immersed brother Philip while he was dying of ALS (see "Prayer" at p. 119) may well be why he lived months, if not years, longer than expected. The same outpouring of love for the Reverend William Sloane Coffin is what may well have kept him alive for three added years, to the surprise of many, after the media reported that his heart was about to quit. The same for Delores Barbeau's longtime partner Carol Olstad, who became fatally ill but live far longer than expected. (Nancy, who was then a justice of the peace, married them in accordance with Vermont law a few weeks before Carol died.) The same for Delores herself.

* * *

When I do a good deed, I feel good. When I truly pray, I feel peace. When I pause to see the beauty of the world, I feel awe and wonder. God is always here. It is I who often wanders.

* * *

Many serious people apparently believe that God has a plan for their lives that they should discern and follow as faithfully as they can. I, on the other hand, do not believe that God has or wants a plan for my life. If God does have one, I am at a loss to discern it. But in gratitude for God's gifts and out of simple decency, I believe I should do what I can to discern and advance God's will for all of us.

* * *

Do I owe my primary allegiance to Quaker principles or to the United States of America? The fact that I would become a conscientiously objector against almost any war I can think of suggests the former; the fact that I would have joined up to stop the Nazis during World War II suggests the latter. In fact, my first allegiance is to my conscience, which the Quaker Way permits. U.S. law does not allow me to object to one war but not another; my conscience requires it.

* * *

Schools should: Give children knowledge of the past, present, and likely future of the Earth, the creatures on it, and the cosmos through which it swings. Teach them to earn an honest living, respect their fellow creatures, delight in their minds and bodies, and grow in compassion. Ignite a passion for learning that will burn throughout their lives.

* * *

While one may educate oneself (become an autodidact), most people don't or can't. It follows that, as much of America seems unaware or not to care, making good schools available for *everyone* is essential for enriching the experience of their lives on Earth—whereas, by chance or design, deteriorating education (no civics course, flawed English, no more diagramming sentences, dependence on calculators, etc.) helps to perpetuate the privilege of the One Percent, who, I'm sure, often say *lay* when they mean *lie*.

* * *

To do its job adequately, a religious school needs to teach the wonders of God's creation that the sciences have uncovered. (Unfortunately this did not occur to me while I was teaching Sunday school back in the 1960s and 1970s.) How can we understand Creation or properly thank God for it if we don't know the readily available facts of how it came to be and how it works?

On the other hand, freedom of religion should mean that public schools need to keep their students free from religiously driven doctrines such as Creationism and the denial of Darwinian evolution—though I think its O.K. to teach those doctrines in Sunday schools, erroneous as they are. If freedom of religion means anything, it means freedom to err.

* * *

Lawyers' perceived willingness to take either side of a case leads to accusations that we pander for pay or are "hired guns," albeit that when conflicts arise, we serve as alternatives to guns. Actually, one of the best things that law school did for me was help me to see and argue either side of a case, that is, to abjure simplistic, judgmental, Manichean views and see that both sides of many cases have their merits. Law school thus helped to open my mind toward feeling compassion for the Other and seeing that there are no Others, only Us.

* * *

Facts are the friends, and doctrine often the foe, of thinking clearly and seeking truth.

* * *

Brother John on July 3, 1995: "Teaching and dissent are equally important." This seems true both for dissent's own sake and for finding the best answers. In terms of Hegel's classic model, teaching is *thesis*, dissent is *antithesis*, and out of the two may grow a *synthesis* that is likely to be sounder than either. Quakers traditionally decide our practical questions by reaching unity or the sense of the Meeting; moving from idea to criticism to synthesis is essentially the way we may (or may not) reach a solution that is often superior to any of the participants' original positions.[xxii]

* * *

Many religiously motivated activists for peace, equality, and justice consider themselves to be hands of God. Presumptuous? I used to think so. But if, as Jesus taught, God favors these values, then the folks who strive for them are doing God's work. Such activists are wont to ask: If not us, who? If not now, when? For much that needs doing, God does not reach a big hand out of the sky and do it for us. If people don't do it, it goes undone. Democracy and true justice only work to the extent that citizens get off their butts. Which has long been too seldom.

* * *

The political and the religious often overlap; and people often cast a cloak of piety over their political agendas, often in all sincerity. That said, God presumably favors peace, equality, and justice, so that folks who strive for these goals are likely to serve as God's instruments. I say "likely" because the best-intentioned people sometimes do more harm than good.

* * *

How does God love us? In part at least, by giving us the ability and will to obey the commandment to love our neighbors, and by letting us feel inner peace—or simply feel good—when we do. We can be the hands of God in many ways, which generally involve loving and, often, getting off our butts.

---

xxii In my limited experience, this method is likely to lead to sound decisions when used by a group, such as many Quaker Meetings, in which the members largely know and trust each other; but it is prone to deadlock when attempted by relative strangers, however well-meaning.

* * *

If there are going to be peace, equality, and justice in this mortal life, they will come when we, the people, bring them on. This awesome responsibility flows from the free will that God gives us. We are only hands of God if we choose to be. God is apparently not willing to degrade us by stepping in and doing it all by God's self, leaving us to sit passively in the bleachers of God's ballpark.

* * *

Morality and logic suggest that Americans who call themselves Christians should pay more heed than most of them seem to the teachings of the Catholic Church about economic justice. Though these teachings have their roots in the Hebrew Bible and the words of Jesus, they coalesced in 1891 with Pope Leo XIII's encyclical *Rerum Novarum: The Condition of Labor.* Pope Pius XI amplified them forty years later; and starting with Pope John XXIII in 1961, they have been amplified considerably as "social teachings," which include the controversial prohibition against abortions and assisted suicide for people in mortal pain. I focus here, though, on the teachings on economic justice, which receive far less attention even as they have, or should have, far more impact on most people's daily lives.

Like the writings of Karl Marx and Charles Dickens, these latter teachings originally responded to the human misery caused by the excesses of unregulated capitalism that accompanied the Industrial Revolution; but unlike Marxism, they did not advocate violent revolution or an unworkable Utopia. So they largely languished. Yet I believe they merit the serious attention of Americans of all faiths and none.

And what are these teachings? While there are valid rights to own property and earn profits, the economy must serve people, not the other way around. Working people, like everyone else, have inherent dignity and a right to food, shelter, rest, health care, and other elements of a decent life.[64] The poor, the hungry, and the stranger merit particular concern. In the words of Pope Benedict XVI, "[T]he primary capital to be safeguarded and valued is…the human person in his or her integrity."[65] As Pope Francis put it in November 2013,

> We can no longer trust in the unseen forces and the invisible hand of the market. Growth in justice requires more than economic growth, while presupposing such growth: it requires decisions, programmes, mechanisms and processes specifically geared to a better distribution of income, the creation of sources

of employment and an integral promotion of the poor which goes beyond a simple welfare mentality.[66]

In sum, people come first—which is a welcome counter to the notion (article of current capitalist faith) that profits come first. There is much more to the teachings, but this much should highlight the contrast between what exists today and what should be. Consider the following:

• Great numbers of migrant farm workers toil long, hot hours for a pittance, many without adequate or any toilets or showers or health care except the occasional shower of poisonous pesticides; they live generation to generation in squalor and ignorance.

• U.S. minimum wages traditionally fall far short of a living wage. There has been some progress here lately.

• Agribusiness floods Mexico with American corn made cheap by subsidies donated willy-nilly by us taxpayers to agribusinesses that don't need them, thus putting vast numbers of *campesinos* out of business and into deep poverty and sometimes on the road to the U.S. border.

• We Americans pay more than twice as much for health care as the Brits, French, Dutch, Germans, Scandinavians, Japanese, or Canadians, yet on average we die sooner than any of them.

• U.S. companies market clothes made on the cheap in Bangladeshi firetraps that have incinerated or collapsed on many hundreds of workers for whom those U.S companies shirk responsibility even as they profit from this sacrifice of foreigners' lives. Adequate safety, after all, cuts profits.

• Improvidently deregulated financial risk-taking, together with rampant mortgage chicanery, by a relatively few people brought on the 2008 financial crisis, with millions of workers forced from their jobs, and many thousands of innocent families forced out of their homes. Nearly none of these crimes were prosecuted.

• Corruption of facts and legislators by fossil fuel interests has blocked all but tardy, inadequate steps towards halting the devastation from people-made climate change. According to the EPA website, the total emissions of CO_2 equivalent in 2021 were 6,340 million metric tons. A single metric ton equals about 2.2 thousand pounds. This vast, continuous diarrhea of human waste mushrooming into the sky has no effect on climate change?

All of the above conduct is wrong, yet it all more or less persists. Correcting each requires a destination—a clear sense of what ought to be—and the initiative to achieve it. Catholic economic teachings go far towards defining sensible, civilized destinations. Who will provide the initiatives needed to move us there?

* * *

"I see nothing wrong with material progress per se, provided people are always given precedence."

—His Holiness the Dalai Lama[67]

* * *

Our natural aversion to making hard choices can obviously be costly. "Thou shalt not kill." But there's an exception for self-defense. Always? If someone had assassinated Hitler in 1936, World War II may well have been averted and the lives of sixty million people saved. Or not. Given Germans' proficiency in battle, the humiliation of their defeat in World War I, and the small-minded, self-indulgently vengeful peace that the leaders of France et al. imposed at the 1919 Versailles peace conference, some other *fuehrer* may well have led Germany into World War II, committed fewer blunders than Hitler, and won the war. So we can only do the best we can to avert tragedy. This seldom means doing nothing.

* * *

"Survival is an incredible privilege. It's also a deep obligation."

— Holocaust survivor Gerda Weissmann Klein.[68]

* * *

"If you're not acting on your beliefs, then they probably aren't real."

—Edward J. Snowden, Hong Kong, 2013.[69]

For me this view is cogent but exaggerated; we have time and money to be activists or even check-writers for only a few of the causes we really believe in.

* * *

There are many ways to serve, and one person can do only so much. People who attempt too much dissipate their energy, crowd their time, and end up doing too little. Not to mention being sometimes frantic. This seems obvious, yet for many well-meaning people, conscience trumps sense, and the goodness of their hearts diminishes the good they do.

* * *

The fact that various religions caught on among partly civilized peoples may already have helped to lift much of the human race out of savagery, though not yet enough and maybe not soon enough. Consider how many clerics still bless the wars of their tribes and nations.

Regarding my phrase "partly civilized peoples": What people are more than partly civilized? As Dostoevsky famously pointed out: "The degree of civilization in a society can be judged by entering its prisons." By that measure, the U.S. scores poorly to miserably.

In an inept effort to combat terrorism after the 9/11 attack, the United States engaged in inflicting agony wholesale, torturing an undisclosed number of suspects to death. Many states still execute certain convicts. We treat many of our prisoners abominably. Prolonged solitary confinement has belatedly been recognized as the torture it is. Many prison systems still won't bother to prevent male inmates from raping other male inmates. (I understand that at least some prisons encourage or tolerate love affairs between female prisoners as a way to keep the peace.)

* * *

Whether we help others may determine whether our own life is full or simply busy.

* * *

People who leave it to God or prayer or other people to cure or forestall the ills of the world shirk their responsibility to their sisters and brothers, to God, and ultimately to themselves.

* * *

It's been the way of the world throughout the ages that people who were exceptionally strong, wily, or lucky have subjugated, exploited, and abused their brothers and sisters of their own tribe and, when they could, other tribes. Recall that it was not pharaohs but workers who built the pyramids. Today the One Percent grow rich; the next 20% do well; the rest don't. But since most people can now communicate better than ever, an era of fairness may eventually open in the U.S to the extent that it has in Scandinavia.

* * *

God gives us life, each other, and the world. What do we give God? We are past the point of burning precious animals on altars, as though such gestures propitiated the animals' Creator. Rather, we give to God when we give to our fellow humans. "Inasmuch as ye have done it unto one of the least of these my brethren, ye have done it unto me." (Matthew 25:40)

* * *

A danger is that people, especially the passionately religious and those burdened with certainty, cast a cloak of piety over their self-serving or harmful or merely political agendas. Thus, by considering ourselves to be hands of God, or acting on the assumption that there's no one but us, we risk being presumptuous, wrong, and hurtful. Before murdering thirteen people and wounding many more in Fort Hood, Texas, in 2009, U.S. Army Major Nidal Malik Hasan reportedly said, "I am going to do God's work."[70] Other deranged fanatics believe much the same. How do we regard John Brown's lethal 1859 raid on Harper's Ferry?

So how does one avoid error yet gain the confidence to act when necessary? Some aids I've found helpful: Pause, reflect, and pray for guidance. Try to discern the promptings of my best self. Consult people I respect, maybe Scriptures and other wisdom that resonate with my best self. Consider the sense of a community I trust. Take my time if I have time to take.

Activism is a chancy business, but it's more likely to go well if I go slowly, get the pertinent facts right, and heed the love, not the anger or urge for vengeance, in my heart.

* * *

Being spiritually faithful, at its best, includes being thoughtful and doing what's needed. As the liberation theology people put it, "Observe, judge, act."

* * *

Legend has it that a stranger walked into a Quaker Meeting, sat down on one of the benches, and waited. Nothing happened. At last, he turned to the person sitting beside him and whispered, "When does the service begin?" The person replied, "This is the Meeting for Worship. The service begins afterwards."

Quakers, of course, don't own the patent on service to others. The truly faithful of every church also serve, as do the people of no church who are faithful to humankind and thus to God.

* * *

The Lord is said to work in mysterious ways. A way that's not mysterious seems to be to work through people who make decisions of conscience and are willing to inconvenience themselves, suffer, and possibly to die as Jesus died, to follow through. Health care workers have done this repeatedly during the Covid pandemic among many other occasions. Firefighters do it.

* * *

Many say that by serving our brothers and sisters, we serve God. Amen.

* * *

"Only by losing your life shall you save it" has many meanings. I like the one that goes, Only by shedding the self-absorption, which served us well as babies, shall we join the human race. Parents can and should, but too often fail to, help their children to do this. Spoiling children stunts their growth as human beings, training them instead to exploit and injure others in the manner of perpetual children. Babies need to exploit others and are usually too inept to injure them. With adults, it's the reverse.

* * *

So why do I scold well-meaning parents in a book of religious reflection? Not because my comments are sound, though I believe they are. Not because spoiled kids irritate me, though they do. (I enjoy most kids.) But because compassion is the highest virtue of the great religions, and self-absorption blocks the path to becoming compassionate. "...Thou shalt love thy neighbor as thyself." (Matthew 22:39)

* * *

The best that parents can do for their children is to instill compassion, right? One way is to set limits on their conduct so that they come to realize that they are not the center of the universe and that other people deserve to be considered. Another way, in which others besides parents may participate, is to introduce them to literature and nourish their love of it, so that they may experience life as other people live it. To this end, Nancy and I gave each of our Jewish granddaughters, upon their Bat Mitzvahs, fine translations of *Crime and Punishment, Anna Karenina, The Brothers Karamazov,* and *War and Peace.* Not that those are the only books or occasions.

* * *

As proof of the pudding is in eating it, proof of the Gospels is in living them.

* * *

In September of 1994, three Catholic nuns and I went on a walking tour of the vast city dump of Matamoros, Mexico, across the Rio Grande from Brownsville, Texas. A few hundred Mexicans—many of whom dwelt in shacks at the edge of the dump or on disused parts of it—were competing with sea gulls, crows, vultures, and lively hogs as they eked out a living by picking through the garbage in this stinking plain of desolation. Now and then, someone would find a human fetus. As we watched, several Evangelical missionaries drove up in a van, and an enthusiastic crowd of the residents gathered around them—obviously a successful ministry to these people in need. But not quite. Our guide told us that when a dump dweller would complain that she'd already borne enough babies, the Evangelicals would tell her that if God wanted her to have another baby, she'd have one. It was Catholic nuns who told her how to prevent unwanted pregnancy. Bravo, sisters!

I cannot believe that God favors the overpopulation that devastates the ecology, helps the well-off to exploit cheap labor, and makes life harder for the dwellers on the Matamoros dump.

* * *

The cheaper the labor, the greater the misery. An on-going sin that has much in common with antebellum slavery, is the life that most of us condemn so many farmworkers to.

* * *

The race may be to the swift and the prize to the strong, but peace comes to the gentle.

* * *

To paraphrase a slur on football coaches, many corporate executives are smart enough to maximize profits and dumb enough to think that matters.

* * *

During my time in the Sanctuary Movement, I would often hear a Guatemalan or Salvadoran refugee praise a person by saying, "He is very humble,' or "She is very humble." How often do you hear Americans praise anyone for being humble? Yet humility opens the door to enriching oneself and letting one see things as they are. Hubris, arrogance, and a sense of entitlement, on the other hand, cloud one's vision and stunt one's growth. "Pride goeth before a fall." "Whom the gods would destroy they first make proud." "...and what does the Lord require of thee, but to do justly, and to love mercy, and to walk humbly with thy God?" (Micah 6:8.)

* * *

The above quote from Micah is the King James Version. The New Revised Standard Version (1989) says "...and what does the Lord require of you but to do justice, and to love kindness, and to walk humbly with your God?" Not an improvement! Whereas occasions for doing *justly* often occur, who among us gets to do *justice* except for our children? *Mercy* includes compassion, *kindness*, and forgiveness—so much richer and warmer than kindness alone.

* * *

Privately funded elections campaigns: Today American food safety, industrial safety, chemical safety, mine safety, and so on are too often a fatal joke. Regulations are too lax and laxly enforced, inspectors are too few, perps are punished far too seldom and lightly, and we the people suffer injury, poisoning, maiming, and death because safety costs profits. It's often more cost-effective to buy legislators than save the limbs and lungs and lives of workers.

Responsible corporations would do well to see that it's in their economic as well as moral interest to push for greater safety enforcement—and for publicly funded election campaigns—lest they be condemned along with the corrupt and corrupting and killing and maiming corporations.

* * *

Most Americans, I fear, don't notice how much corruption infests this nation or can't be bothered to do anything about it.

* * *

How free is our free will if we are forever guiding our decisions by what we think Jesus would do in this or that situation? Quite restricted, I think, though freer than we may suppose. On the other hand, how free are we if we do mainly what we feel like? With sex, drugs, and other instant gratifications? Self-indulgence often confines us to the bondage of ignorance and poverty.

* * *

What happened to the notion that virtue is its own reward? While we can't know whether there is divine justice, it seems to exist to the extent that people tend to be happy when they live right and hollow when they don't.

* * *

The first and perhaps hardest part of loving my neighbors as myself is realizing that all of those neighbors and strangers are as human as I am. A culture that fosters individualism, greed, consumerism, competition, impatience, and mundane success—and puts little value on humility and the quaint notion that enough is enough—must make it hard to realize this fact. It's hard to be a good Christian (or a good anyone) if one espouses the pure (raw) capitalist faith that the race is to the swift and the Devil take the hindmost.

* * *

For the sake of the Earth and everybody on it including the wealthy, we must have an economy whose health does not depend on constant growth. This is obvious but still heresy.

* * *

We demean the gift of life and may fritter it away if we expend it in striving to reach a perceived pinnacle of wealth or power. On the other hand, if striving to do one's best happens to bring one to such a pinnacle, so be it. Someone has to be there, though it may be a bit lonely. A better place for most people, including Nancy and me, is to be in the fellowship of the middle range. Jesus and many of today's most admirable missionaries have exercised "a preferential option for the poor" and chose the bottom. The ones I know seem satisfied and happy.

* * *

Which question shall we ask from the grave: Was I rich or powerful or famous? Was I loving to my family, kind to everyone I knew, and helpful to people in need?

* * *

Perhaps the most important spiritual decision that one makes (or not) from time to time: How shall I spend the rest of my life?

* * *

Sister Helen Prejean, who has long been a leader in the campaign to end capital punishment, built a spirited seminar at the annual demonstration to close the School of the Americas (School of Assassins) in Fort Benning at Columbus, Georgia, in November 2006 around two questions: "What awakened you to justice?" and "What feeds your spirituality?"

* * *

"Don't, for God's sake, ever earn more than you need to live on. Try not to be too successful."
— John Held, Jr., the brilliant illustrator of Jazz Age America, a.k.a., the Roaring '20s.[71] While Held may have overstated it, you probably see his point.

* * *

There are two ways to be rich: accumulate much, and want little.

* * *

Shall I remain in the thrall of a desire to prove myself superior, or simply see myself as a flawed but worthy member of the fellowship of humankind?

* * *

Deciding what doesn't matter surely helps to unclutter one's closet and life.

* * *

People and nations commonly convince themselves that they fight only in self-defense wars. This just war commonly means just this war.

* * *

Though war is nearly always a grievous mistake, violent self-defense may be necessary. Hitler had to be stopped, as many Quakers agreed at the time, notwithstanding their commitment to peace. Like the Romans of old and countless other aggressors, Hitler told his people that his attacks were defensive, and most Germans are said to have found it easy to believe him, not, I suppose, because they were Germans or stupid, but because they were human. How many Americans know that many Iranians hate us because we overthrew their democracy in 1953 and installed a regime that kept order for the next quarter century by the tortures and murders of SAVAK, the dreaded, CIA-instructed Iranian secret police?

* * *

Thousands of American youngsters keep on dying in wars that America need not have fought, from Vietnam to Afghanistan and Iraq and wars before and between. Did they die in vain? For me as a veteran of the U.S. Army (though not of combat), the answer is a resounding No! One of the noblest and most generous ways that people can die is for their comrades and their country, and this is true whether or not the war that killed them was a stupid mistake.

But in return, we, their countrymen, owe it to them to do the very best we can to assure that our country does *not* enter ill-advised wars. In this we often fail. See above. Young men and women who join the armed services are willing to, and often do, sacrifice their lives or various parts of their bodies or minds for us. What sacrifices are we willing to make to assure that they don't suffer or die unless absolutely necessary? Obviously not yet enough.

* * *

To the extent that we Americans concern ourselves with "success," we may hesitate to work for peace or justice where we see little or no likelihood of succeeding. But it is said, soundly I believe, that we are called not to be successful but to be faithful. Which may create the best chance for succeeding against the odds. As the fearless Italian journalist (and partisan during World War II), Oriana Fallaci said, only slight exaggerating, "In the history of the world those who have won have always been those who challenged the unchallengeable."[72]

* * *

During the Hitler years, a German woman repeatedly risked her life to spirit Jews from Germany into Holland (before it was occupied). One of them asked her, Why are you doing this for me, a complete stranger? The German replied, "Because I don't want to be ashamed of myself when I come to stand before my God."[73]

* * *

A guide to personal conduct called "Situation Ethics," which became popular during the 1960s, asked people to do the most loving thing under the circumstances at hand. Yet if traditional rules are thus relaxed, it becomes a challenge to sort out the sensible from the self-indulgent. In practice, Situation Ethics often led relative strangers to screw, which they took to be "the most loving thing" in the warmth of the moment, and later to feel they'd been screwed.

* * *

Maybe more sensible and less permissive: Do what is loving, *right, and just* under the circumstances at hand. If it's not right and just, it may not be as loving as one feels, especially if one feels horny.

* * *

If the United States practiced "Situation Peace," that is, did the most non-violent thing in each situation, would the rest of the world be (a) astounded, (b) incredulous, (c) relieved, (d) safer, (e) all of the above?

* * *

America has globalized business far more effectively than it has globalized compassion.

* * *

A Golden Rule for America: Intervene in other nations as we would have them intervene in us. I don't see this happening soon, but like to imagine a world in which it's common.

* * *

Karen Armstrong's Charter for Compassion (Appendix A) draws a connection between compassion and the Golden Rule. Indeed, I think the two are holding hands.

* * *

If you want to make the world a better place, you are considered good; but if you want to make your society more just, you are suspect. The humble, valiant Brazilian cleric Dom Hélder Câmara famously observed, "When I fed the poor, they called me a saint. When I asked why they are poor, they called me a communist."[74]

* * *

My dear niece Suzanne Greene McLone sees a parallel between Dom Hélder and the 9/11 attack on America: "When I condemned this mass murder, they called me a patriot. When I asked what we may have done to provoke it, they called me disloyal."[xxiii]

* * *

I can't read music, much less write it, and I know that a Christmas carol requires that rare gem, a timeless tune, if it's going to catch on in churches and shopping malls. The lyrics to "What Child Is This?" have fit the timeless tune of "Greensleeves" ever since William Chatterton Dix wrote them in 1865. With all his in mind, I have written lyrics which I call "Song of the Star," which fit the timeless tune called "Love Is Blue," and which are in Appendix C. I hope they will give people pleasure as they worship or shop.

* * *

We are tourists passing through this Earth on a one-way ticket, as far as we know. We're here today and gone tomorrow. Best to do the best we can and hope for the best hereafter.

* * *

While we cannot know all the answers about the cosmos or very many about God, we know, if we wish to, how to live fully, peacefully, and helpfully.

* * *

When my daughter Erin was a little girl, she put her red and blue pencils to a sheet of paper and made a sign for our home: "Everyone who enters here must have love."

* * *

Nancy, in her seventies: "We should never lose the little kid within us."

---

xxiii According to the prompt analysis of then President George W. Bush, the attackers hated us for our freedoms. To the extent that there may be merit in his hasty analysis, I understand that the hatred arose, not from the freedom of speech and religion and so on, but from our freedoms meaning our perceived licentiousness.

Appendix A

Charter for Compassion

The principle of compassion lies at the heart of all religious, ethical and spiritual traditions, calling us always to treat all others as we wish to be treated ourselves. Compassion impels us to work tirelessly to alleviate the suffering of our fellow creatures, to dethrone ourselves from the centre of our world and put another there, and to honour the inviolable sanctity of every single human being, treating everybody, without exception, with absolute justice, equity and respect.

It is also necessary in both public and private life to refrain consistently and empathically from inflicting pain. To act or speak violently out of spite, chauvinism, or self-interest, to impoverish, exploit or deny basic rights to anybody, and to incite hatred by denigrating others—even our enemies—is a denial of our common humanity. We acknowledge that we have failed to live compassionately and that some have even increased the sum of human misery in the name of religion.

We therefore call upon all men and women to restore compassion to the centre of morality and religion

- to return to the ancient principle that any interpretation of scripture that breeds violence, hatred or disdain is illegitimate
- to ensure that youth are given accurate and respectful information about other traditions, religions and cultures
- to encourage a positive appreciation of cultural and religious diversity
- to cultivate an informed empathy with the suffering of all human beings
- even those regarded as enemies.

We urgently need to make compassion a clear, luminous and dynamic force in our polarized world. Rooted in a principled determination to transcend selfishness, compassion can break down political, dogmatic, ideological and religious boundaries. Born of our deep interdependence, compassion is essential to human relationships and to a fulfilled humanity. It is the path to enlightenment, and indispensable to the creation of a just economy and a peaceful global community.[76]

Appendix B

WALK IN FREEDOM
(To the tune of the "Battle Hymn of the Republic")

I

We came here through Alaska and across the tossing sea,
From Asia and from Africa and Europe's family.
Some came in hope and some in chains, all longing to be free,
Across this wondrous land.

> Let the people walk in freedom,
> Let the people walk in freedom,
> Let the people walk in freedom,
> Across this wondrous land.

II

Through forests and through prairies with a beauty yet untold,
We took the chance to prove ourselves with labor, land, and gold,
And find a place to live and love and peacefully grow old,
Across this fruitful land.

> Let the people stand for justice,
> Let the people stand for justice,
> Let the people stand for justice,
> Across this fruitful land.

III

Like canyons red and cities white and mountains' haze of blue,
And golden corn in Iowa beneath the morning dew,
Our skins have varied colors, but our blood's the human hue,
Across this blessed land.

> Let the people cherish freedom,
> Let the people cherish freedom,
> Let the people cherish freedom,
> Across this blessed land.

Appendix C

SONG OF THE STAR
(To the Tune of "Love Is Blue")

I

Star shine, the wise men lead,
Their wisdom less than love for a child.
Christ, Christ, of Mary born
Light our way, no longer forlorn.

> Star long dark over fig and palm
> Lead us now to know thy calm.

II

Fear, fear, the shepherds dread.
Fear not God, the angel said.
Hide, hide, when light first shines,
Truth so bright it leaves us blind.
> Proud stand alone and dare not fear
> Till the peace of God is here.

III

Christ, Christ the Lord is come
To tell the world that God is love.
Live, live now as before.
Show every soul what life is for.
> Born of yore yet never born.
> We heed not and go on as before.

IV

Live, live in every heart.
Doubt and sin forever depart.
Strong, strong yet like a dove
Calm our flame, O fire of love.
> Guide of kings, guide us now, we pray,
> Born in us, light our own Christmas day.

Endnotes

1 Australia Yearly Meeting puts it well: "A testimony is neither a rule nor a creed. It is both an ideal to strive for and a way for our lives to speak."

2 *When Bad Things Happen to Good People* (Avon Books, 1983), pp. 142-143.

3 In an interview by Krista Tippett on National Public Radio, March 7, 2010.

4 Dennis Overbye, "Kepler, the Little NASA Spacecraft That Could, No Longer Can," *New York Times*, October 30, 2018.

5 *Is There a God?* (Oxford University Press, rev. ed., 2010), pp. 40, 48.

6 In *Pygmalion*, Act V (Pocket Books, 2001), p. 135.

7 https://www.nationalgeographic.org/media/wolves-yellowstone/

8 Dianna Ortiz and Patricia Davis, *The Blindfold's Eyes: My Journey from Torture to Truth* (Orbis Books, 2002).

9 In *Is There a God?, op. cit.*, p. 56.

10 Scholar of Judaism Daniel Ross Goodman discussed this theory in his article, "A Biblical Theory Illuminated," in the Winter/Spring 2014 issue of the *Harvard Divinity Bulletin*. Piquantly, he suggested that God's alleged courtship of the ancient Hebrews is analogous to Jay Gatsby's courtship of Daisy Buchanan in F. Scott Fitzgerald's, *The Great Gatsby*. A more apt analogy, I suggest, is that people who espouse this theory are like the flea floating down the river on his back and signaling for the drawbridge to be raised because he has an erection.

11 *Why Religion Matters: The Fate of the Human Spirit in an Age of Disbelief* (HarperSanFrancisco, 2001), pp. 191-192.

12 In *The Case for God* (Anchor Books, 2010), pp. 122, 178.

13 See Krista Tippett, *Einstein's God: Conversations About Science and the Human Spirit* (Penguin Books, 2010), pp. 20-24.

14 Tippitt, *op. cit.*, pp. 35-36.

15 Tippitt, *op. cit.*, p.22.

16 Sept. 8, 2003, *New Yorker*, pp. 42–43.

17 Lisa Randall, *Higgs Discovery: The Power of Empty Space* (The Bodley Head, London, 2012), p 47.

18 Richard Dawkins, *The God Delusion* (Houghton Mifflin Company, 2006), p.145.

19 Published by Twelve in 2007.

20 Dawkins *op. cit.*, pp. 171, 188. Dawkins notes, pp. 169-170, "Physicists have calculated that, if the laws and constants of physics had been even slightly different, the universe would have developed in such a way that life would have been impossible." Still, Dawkins's inability to explain the existence of God—especially the complex God it likely took to create this complex universe—leads him to conclude that God doesn't exist and certainly has not existed forever, yet he is unsure what other first cause there might be.

21 In *The Whole Shebang* (Simon & Schuster, paper, 1998), pp. 304-305.

22 Basic Books, 2000, pp. 3-4, 166-167. It is worth noting that Rees, unlike Hitchens and Dawkins, is respectful and not derisive towards people and faiths he disagrees with.

23 See Tippett, in loc. cit.

24 "The Study of Religion on the Other Side of Disgust" in the Spring/Summer 2019 issue.

25 In *The Post-American World* (W. W. Norton, 2008), p. 156.

26 In "A Human Approach to World Peace" in *Journal of Human Values*, 18, 2 (2012), p. 95-96.

27 Maybe fifteen of us from Wilton (CT) Friends Meeting were off on a weekend retreat to learn about liberation theology. Our instructor, Ulises Torres, was a Methodist minister who had been tortured in Chile and sent into exile following the 1973 CIA-backed coup there that led to the death of elected President Salvador Allende and the brutal regime of Augusto Pinochet. Ulises's crime? He and his wife had been renting a room to a labor leader, but as Ulises explained, they couldn't evict their tenant on account of a right-wing coup. He asked us to write down our interpretations of several passages in the Gospels. Then he read to us what several Nicaraguan campesinos had said about the same passages, as recorded in Ernesto Cardenal's *The Gospel in Solentiname, Volume 2* (Orbis Books, 1985). He recommended this volume as the best of the four. The meanings that we Connecticut Quakers drew were fairly similar to each other's and strikingly different from those of the campesinos.

28 See, e.g., Bart D. Ehrman, *Misquoting Jesus: The Story Behind Who Changed the Bible and Why* (Harper/Collins, 2005)

29 William Howard Melish, *Strength through Struggle: Christian Social Witness in the Crucible of these Times* (The Bromwell Press, 1953), p. 48.

30 Quoted from Harold S. Kushner, *Nine Essential Things I've Learned About Life* (Knopf, 2015), pp. 160–162.

31 Interview by John McKenna, RTE Ireland, May 9 & 12, 1988.

32 In the version certified in 1929, pp. 15-16.

33 Garry Wills, *What the Qur'an Meant and Why It Matters* (Viking, 2017), pp. 119, 121.

34 The poll was of 2002 adults and conducted by the Public Religion Research Institute and the Brookings Institution, as reported in the August 2–15, 2013, *National Catholic Reporter*.

35 See Matthew 25:40, 45.

36 In the March 12–26 *National Catholic Reporter*, p. 25. Father Coyne is the author of *The Theology of Fear* (CreateSpace, 2012).

37 Ben Pink Dandelion, *Celebrating the Quaker Way* (Quaker Books, 2009), p. 10.

38 As quoted by Margaret Hope Bacon in *The Quiet Rebels: The Story of Quakers in America* (Pendle Hill Publications, 1999), p. 12.

39 *What the Qur'an Meant, op. cit.*, p. 213.

40 As quoted in Eben Alexander, *Proof of Heaven* (Simon & Schuster, 2012), p. 147.

41 *When Bad Things Happen to Good People* (Avon Books, 1983), *op. cit.*, p. 57.

42 As quoted in Jonathan Montaldo and Robert G. Toth, eds., *Bridges to Contemplative Living with Thomas Merton, Vol. Two: Becoming Who You Already Are* (Ave Maria Press, 2010), p. 20.

43 His Holiness the Dalai Lama, *An Appeal to the World: The Way to Peace in a Time of Division* (William Morrow, 2017), p. 100.

44 Schocken Books, 1981; Avon Books, 1983; Anchor Books, 2004.

45 Rabbi Hillel is quoted on pages xvii and 59, above.

46 *Faith and Practice of New England Yearly Meeting of Friends*, written and self-published by that yearly meeting, 1985, pp. 206, 212. The last sentence adapts words of George Fox, who founded Quakerism in the mid-Seventeenth Century.

47 Carole Gallagher in her book, *The Irish Potato Famine* (Chelsea House Publishers, 2002), pp. 96-97.

48 In *The New York Times* online, April 15, 2020.

49 James Pott & Company, 1929, pp. 6 and 23.

50 Image, 2000. Another sermon-in-a-title is Mary Robinson's *Everybody Matters* (Blooms-bury USA, 2014).

51 Ta-Nehisi Coates, *We Were Eight Years in Power* (One World, , 2017), p. 110.

52 *How We Die: Reflections on Life's Final Chapter* (Knopf, 1994) was a *New York Times* bestseller, winner of the non-fiction National Book Award, and a finalist for a Pulitzer Prize.

53 Peter L. Bergen, *The Longest War: The Enduring Conflict between America and al-Qae-da* (Free Press, 2011), pp. 17-24.

54 *An Appeal, op. cit.*, p. 97.

55 The book's subtitle is *Nuclear Weapons, the Damascus Accident, and the Illusion of Safety.* Penguin published it. The review was in the September 30, 2013, *New Yorker*, quoted at pages 79–80. Menand teaches literature and American cultural history at Harvard, and frequently writes for that magazine.

56 Craig Lambert, "Nuclear Weapons or Democracy," *Harvard Magazine*, March-April, 2014.

57 March–April 2014 issue, pp. 47, 49-51.

58 As quoted in the *New York Times Book Review*, June 18, 2017, p.18.

59 As quoted by Fareed Zakaria in his review of *The Kennan Diaries* (Frank Castigliola, ed., W. W. Norton, 2014), in the Feb. 23, 2014, *New York Times Book Review*.

60 In a letter to the editor in the May–June 2014 *Harvard Magazine* written in response to its above-cited "Nuclear Weapons or Democracy" article. Pravica identifies himself as a physicist, activist, and a Harvard Ph.D.

61 *An Appeal, op. cit.*, p. 91.

62 The Penguin Press, 2009.

63 From his Minister's Minute of April 8, 1988, as quoted in his book *Three Islands in My Life and Ministry* (Neponset River Press, 2013), pp. 285-286.

64 Much of this summary paraphrases the website of the United States Conference of Catholic Bishops on Catholic Social Teaching, as of July 23, 2014. A handy place to learn more about these Catholic teachings is a pastoral letter (a 188-page paperback) called *Economic Justice for All,* first published by the National Conference of Catholic Bishops in 1986. For the more ambitious, there is David J. O'Brien and Thomas A. Shannon, eds., *Catholic Social Thought: The Documentary Heritage, Expanded Edition* (Orbis Books, 2010, 816 pages), which I have so far only dipped into.

65 In his 2009 encyclical *Caritas in Veritate: On the Integral Human Development in Charity and Truth*, #25.

66 Apostolic Exhortation Evangelii Gaudium (Joy of the Gospel) of the Holy Father Fran-cis, November 24, 2013, # 204.

67 *An Appeal, op. cit.*, p. 99.

68 On the *PBS News Hour*, May 2, 2012.

69 As quoted by Glenn Greenwald in *No Place to Hide: Edward Snowden, the NSA, and the U.S. Surveillance State* (Metropolitan Books, Henry Holt, 2014), p. 45.

70 Quoted in Peter L. Bergen, *The Longest War* (Free Press, 2011), p. 17–24.

71 As quoted in the Dec. 6, 1987 *New York Times Book Review*, p. 14.

72 In her book, *Interview with History* (Houghton Mifflin, 1976), p. 303.

73 Bernt Engelmann in his book, *In Hitler's Germany* (Pantheon, 1976, paper, 1978), p. 85.

74 The quote is sometimes attributed to Saint Oscar Romero. Which is not to say that Romero did not say it or quote it.

75 As copied on March 12, 2014, from http://charterforcompassion.org/the-charter.

Acknowledgments

I heartily thank these generous people for their contributions on behalf of this volume:

Peter Nagel, Phil Megna, Mary Eagleson, James Lumsden, Len and Mary Ann Cadwallader, Peter Areson, Carl Buffum, Dave Martin, Ted Day, Michael Barszewski, Andrew Thompson, Michael Morfit, and my brother Richard for their support and approval of the book in spite of their varying disagreements with it.

Nearly half the people who wrote the kind comments at the front of the book are Quakers and nearly half are Catholics. If their comments were unsigned, I would be hard pressed to guess the faiths of their authors, and perhaps you would be too. Is there a lesson here about the spirituality of thoughtful people or the kindness of spiritual people?

More than half a century ago, James Lumsden was my most challenging Sunday school student; and he and I remained close friends thereafter. The hour I remember best came on the Sunday he brought to class the new Crosby, Stills, Nash & Young *Déjà Vu* album, my lesson plan evaporated, and we spent the hour listening to the LP and discussing the lyrics, especially the poignant "Teach Your Children."

Sister Bernadette Bostwick for permission to use her inspired icon on the cover.

Kitty Werner for her artistry, expertise, patience and advice in designing the book and its cover and shepherding me through this, my second self-publishing venture. Were it not for her, this book, like my novel *Roses in the Night*, would still be only a file on my MacBook.

And as always, my wife Nancy Bell for remaining my number one inspiration and critic.

About the Author

Malcolm Bell grew up in Brooklyn, served in the U.S. Army, and practiced law in Manhattan before the state and federal courts of New York. He wrote *The Turkey Shoot: Tracking the Attica Cover-up* (Grove Press 1985), reissued as *The Attica Turkey Shoot: Carnage, Cover-up and the Pursuit of Justice*, (Skyhorse Publishing, 2017, paperback 2022), which tells of being a New York State prosecutor who was assigned to indict police for the murders and other violent felonies they committed during the 1971 Attica prison riot, then was blocked from finishing the job. He resigned in protest and took the cover-up public in the *New York Times*, leading to revelations that high State officials had sought to suppress and to more justice than they found convenient.

While becoming a confirmed Episcopalian at age thirteen, he began to question traditional Christian doctrines. His spiritual journey took him from the Episcopal Church to a United Church of Christ, where he taught junior and senior high Sunday school, to the Religious Society of Friends (Quakers), where he found his spiritual home. In the 1980s, he became active in the Sanctuary Movement and, as a matter of conscience, broke the law to stand with illegal refugees fleeing the state-led, U.S.-backed terror in Guatemala and El Salvador. He wrote about the Guatemalan civil war in his novel, *Roses in the Night*.

He has long engaged in spiritual discussions in groups where he or he and his wife Nancy were the only Quakers. For the past forty years, he has jotted down his spiritual thoughts; they comprise this book. Today he lives with Nancy among the Green Mountains of Vermont, where he continues to write.